SPANISH 1

PART 2

Kathleen E. Talipan

Julie M. Glenz

SPANISH 1 PART 2

ISBN 978-1-933387-60-4

Published by Quantum Scientific Publishing a division of Sentient Enterprises, Inc. Pittsburgh, PA. Copyright © 2007 by Sentient Enterprises, Inc. All rights reserved.

Printed in the United States of America

10 9 8 7 6 5 4 3 2 1

Quantum Scientific Publishing

Cover design by Scott Sheariss
Images courtesy of Brian Saltzer and the stock.xchng website.

Inside layouts by Bob Baker

Lincoln Interactive is dedicated to helping schools meet the demands of 21st century learners. Designing, developing, and delivering high-quality curriculum that makes innovative and effective educational experiences available anywhere, Lincoln Interactive is offering schools and communities cutting-edge strategies for creating and sustaining academic excellence.

The Lincoln curriculum is one of the first comprehensive elementary through high school series developed exclusively for online learning . This innovative, challenging, standards - based and peer - reviewed coursework is available to any school seeking to enhance and expand its educational services. Lincoln Interactive offers a full slate of both basic and advanced courses.

Lincoln Interactive is truly a 21st Century curriculum choice that provides engaging student centered educational experiences. Formatted to a unique and consistent design model, Lincoln Interactive courses offer flexibility in scheduling, a variety of course content, and regular feedback from highly trained, certified teachers. Each course provides experiences in varying learning styles. Multiple levels of interaction are available to students allowing them to receive as little assistance as they want or as much help as they need to succeed. Pod casts, streaming video, illustrations, songs, and gaming simulations create truly engaging and interactive lessons.

The Lincoln Interactive Curriculum is comprised of student friendly courses with a wide range of opportunities for academic mastery, investigation, and interaction.

CONTENTS

UNIT 1

MY NEIGHBORHOOD

UNIT 2

AT SCHOOL

UNIT 3

FOOD

UNIT 4

CLOTHING AND SHOPPING

APPENDICES

SPANISH 1

PART 2

MY NEIGHBORHOOD

SECTION 1.1 - LOCATION

■ DAY 1

You will learn:
- To list basic direction/location words
- To state the basic location of one item
- To ask the basic location of one item

Location

When you give the location of something or someone, you state where that person or thing is. For example, if you wanted to tell your location, you would probably say that you are at your house, in your room, or in front of your computer. In stating this, you are giving your temporary placement. In this lesson you will be able to state and ask the basic location of an item.

Vocabulary related to Location/Direction

A la derecha (de)*	to the left of
A la izquierda (de)	to the right of
Al lado (de)	next to; to the side of
Cerca (de)	near; close to
Debajo (de)	under; beneath
Delante (de)	in front of
Detrás (de)	behind; in back of
En*	in; at; on
Encima (de)	on top of
Enfrente (de)	in front of
Entre	between
Lejos (de)	far from
Aquí	here
Allí	there
Allá	over there (farther than "allí")

* = Words in parentheses are used when the vocabulary is part of a prepositional phrase.

Questions and Responce

The question word for "where?" is "¿dónde?" in Spanish. Anytime you want to ask the location of an item, you can form a question using "¿dónde?" The following examples will model the question formation.

¿Dónde está la mochila?	Where is the book bag?
¿Dónde está la revista?	Where is the magazine?
¿Dónde están las chicas?	Where are the girls?

Responses:

La mochila está aquí.	The book bag is here.
La revista está a la derecha.	The magazine is to the right.
Las chicas están cerca.	The girls are close.

■ DAY 2

OBJECTIVES

You will learn to:

- To state basic location of people and items
- To ask the basic location of people and items
- To give the location of the capital city of Spain
- To list some facts about the capital city of Spain

Location

In the last section, you learned basic vocabulary to give the location of an item or a person. In this lesson, you will continue to apply that vocabulary so that you will be able to say the location of more than one item or person.

You will use the interrogative word "¿dónde?" plus the appropriate verb to ask a question. Let's look at an example:

¿Dónde están el televisor y el estéreo?
Where are the television and the stereo?

Están aquí.
They are here.

A review of the verb "estar" will show you the different conjugations to use with the location of items or people. Don't forget- when you are asking where one thing or person is, use "está." If you want to ask about one or more people/things, you will need to use "están."

Review of Estar

Estar- to be (is, am, are)

Yo	estoy- I am	Nosotros Nosotras	estamos- We are
Tú	estás- You are	Vosotros Vosotras	estáis- All of you are
Él Ella Usted (Ud.)	está- He is She is You (formal) are	Ellos Ellas Ustedes (Uds.)	están- They are All of you are

Examples

¿Dónde estamos?   Where are we?
Estamos en Florida.   We are in Florida.

¿Dónde estás?   Where are you?
Estoy en casa.   I am at home.

¿Dónde están los profesores? Where are the teachers?
Los profesores están allá.   The teachers are over there.

 Nota Cultural

Madrid

¿Dónde está Madrid?

Madrid está en España.

Did you know that Madrid is the capital of Spain?

It is also...

- Located in the center of the Iberian Peninsula and Spain.
- Situated geographically more westward than London.
- The third most populated city in the European Union.
- Madrid is one of the most exciting cities in Europe.

Ejercicios

Exercise 1.1a:

Directions: Translate the statements.

1. El cartel está a la derecha del escritorio.   _____
2. El armario está lejos del cartel.   _____
3. El zapato está debajo de la cama.   _____
4. El reloj está al lado del televisor.   _____
5. El televisor está encima del escritorio.   _____
6. La cama está entre el armario y el escritorio.   _____
7. La cama está a la izquierda del reloj.   _____
8. El cartel está en el cuarto.   _____
9. El escritorio está delante de la cama.   _____
10. El cartel está cerca del televisor.   _____

Exercise 1.1b:

Directions: You need to locate the following items at your house. Ask where each of the items is located in Spanish.

1. The clothes_____

2. The table _____

3. The rug _____

4. The lamp_____

5. The window _____

Ejercicios

Exercise 1.1c:

Directions: Based on what you read, draw in the item based on the order below.

1. La alfombra está debajo.
2. La cama está encima.
3. La lámpara está a la izquierda.
4. La ventana está a la derecha.
5. La puerta está al lado.
6. La silla está enfrente.

Exercise 1.1d:

Directions: Fill in the sentence with the correct conjugation of "estar."

1. Yo _____ allí.
2. Nosotros _____ lejos de California.
3. Miguel _____ encima de la silla.
4. Los estéreos _____ en mi casa.
5. Uds. _____ aquí.
6. ¿Dónde _____ tú?

Ejercicios

Exercise 1.1e:

Directions: Position yourself in relation to a table at your house.

1. Estás cerca de la mesa.
2. Estás lejos de la mesa.
3. Estás debajo de la mesa.
4. Estás encima de la mesa.
5. Estás al lado de la mesa.

Exercise 1.1f:

Directions: Write it out in Spanish.

1. I am not here. _____

2. You are not there! _____

3. We are in Costa Rica. _____

4. The chairs are next to the table. _____

5. The clock is next to the window. _____

6. Where are all of you? _____

SECTION 1.2 - PLACES IN A TOWN OR CITY

■ DAY 1

OBJECTIVES

You will learn to:

- To list places in a town or city
- To demonstrate an understanding of place location

Places in a Town or City

In the last section, you learned how to state and ask about location. An extension of that is to learn the names of places in your town or city so that you can state, give and ask for their location.

Places in a Town or City

El banco	the bank
La biblioteca	the library
La casa	the house
El cine	the movie theater
El centro comercial	the mall
El correo*	the post office
La escuela	the school
El gimnasio	the gymnasium (gym)
El hotel	the hotel
El hospital	the hospital
El museo	the museum
El parque	the park
La piscina	the pool
La plaza	the center of town
El restaurante	the restaurant
El supermercado	the supermarket
La tienda	the store
El trabajo	the work

*Instead of "el correo," you may also see simply "correos" to refer to the post office.

Places of Worship

La iglesia	the church
La mezquita	the mosque
La sinagoga	the synagogue
El templo	the temple or place of worship

■ Day 2

OBJECTIVES

You will learn to:

- − To state location of places in relation to other places
- − To ask location of places in relation to other places
- − To demonstrate a comprehension for La Plaza Mayor in Madrid

Location – Using "del" and "de la"

Often the location of an item, person, or place is given in relation to something else. For example, if someone were to ask the location of the store, a possible response could be that it is next to the supermarket.

In order to be able to give the location of an item, person, or place in relation to something else, the following pattern needs to be used. When the "de" of the location word is followed by "el" it needs to be combined to form the contraction "del."

Incorrect:	El parque está al lado **de el** cine.
Correct:	El parque está al lado **del** cine.
Meaning:	The park is next to the movie theater.

However, if the "de" of the location word is followed by "la" there is no combination.

Correct:	El parque está al lado de la casa.
Meaning:	The park is next to the house.

 Nota Cultural

La Plaza Mayor

In the Spain's capital city of Madrid, there are many plazas. A plaza is an open area in an urban center often equated to a city square.

The Plaza Mayor is the central plaza in Madrid and a well-known landmark to people all over the world. It is surrounded by building and has 9 entranceways. It is the often the site of cafés and markets.

Ejercicios

Exercise 1.2a:

Directions: Based on the scenario, write in the place you would go.

1. You and your family are going out to eat. _____

2. You and your friends want to go shopping. _____

3. You need to mail a package. _____

4. You want to see a movie. _____

5. You are going to borrow some books. _____

6. You need to go grocery shopping. _____

7. You need a workout. _____

8. You and your friends are going swimming. _____

9. You need to go for a check-up. _____

10. You need to go home after a long day. _____

Exercise 1.2b:

Directions: Name where the people of the following religions would worship.

1. Los católicos están en la _____.
2. Los cristianos están en el _____.
3. Los musulmanes están en la _____.
4. Los judíos están en la _____.

Exercise 1.2c:

Directions: Draw a picture of the place where Miguel is.

1. Miguel está en el supermercado.
2. Miguel está en el banco.
3. Miguel está en el centro comercial.
4. Miguel está en la iglesia.
5. Miguel está en el correo.

1.   2.   3.

4.   5.

Ejercicios

Exercise 1.2d:

Directions: Fill in the blank with "del," "de la" or nothing.

1. Nosotros estamos cerca _____ del banco.
2. Mi casa está lejos _____ escuela.
3. Ignacio está _____ aquí.
4. Las tiendas están a la derecha _____ parque.
5. Estás _____ en el cine.
6. El templo está a la izquierda _____ biblioteca.
7. La piscina está detrás _____ casa.
8. La biblioteca está muy cerca _____ correo.

Exercises 1.2e:

Directions: Place the buildings in town.

1. La plaza está en el centro.
2. El museo está a la izquierda de la plaza.
3. La tienda está a la derecha de la plaza.
4. La piscina está en la piscina.
5. El gimnasio está enfrente de la plaza.
6. La escuela está detrás de la plaza.

El Pueblo- Town

Exercise 1.2f:

Directions: Ask the following questions. Follow the example.

Example: Is the house near the bank?   ¿Está la casa cerca del banco?

1. Is the store near the library? _____

2. Is the gym far from the house? _____

3. Is the mosque next to the restaurant? _____

4. Are the movie theaters behind the mall?_____

5. Are my friends in front of the school? _____

SECTION 1.3 - THINGS TO DO IN TOWN

■ DAY 1

OBJECTIVES

You will learn:

− To list a purpose for being at a place

− To state what you do or like to do at location

− To ask what you do or like to do at location

Things To Do In Town

It is common to be at a certain place in your town or city for a purpose. You may like what goes on at that place. For example, if you like to watch movies, you may always be at the theater. Or, you may need to conduct business at an establishment. If you needed to borrow a book, you would be at the library. The following vocabulary will allow you to provide a purpose for your presence at various places in your town or city.

New Vocabulary

Ahorrar	to save
Bajar información	to download information
Enviar por correo	to send through the mail
Quedarse la noche	to stay overnight
Ir de compras	to go shopping
Prestar	to borrow
Rezar	to pray
Tener un examen médico	to have a medical exam
Navegar en Internet	to surf the internet
Ver una película	to see a movie
Ver una exposición	to see an exhibit

Review Vocabulary

Aprender	to learn
Pasear el perro	to walk the dog
Comer y beber	to eat and drink
Comprar cosas	to buy things
Correr	to run
Estudiar	to study
Hacer ejercicios	to do exercises
Practicar deportes	to play sports
Levantar pesos	to lift weights
Nadar	to swim
Pasar tiempo con amigos	to spend time with friends
Trabajar	to work

■ DAY 2

You will learn to:

- To state when others do or like to do at location
- To ask when you do or like to do at location

When

You may state your action at you location with the use of the word "cuando" which means "when" in Spanish.

Cuando estoy en el cine, yo veo una película.
When I am at the movie theater, I see a movie.

Cuando estamos en la piscina, nadamos.
When we are in/at the pool, we swim/are swimming.

Estoy en el gimnasio cuando hago ejercicios.
I am at the gym when I exercise.

To ask location questions with "when," you can follow the examples below. Don't forget to use the accent on the "á" in "¿cuándo?" when asking questions.

¿Cuándo ves películas?
When do you see movies?

¿Cuándo nadan Uds.?
When do all of you swim?

¿Cuándo estás en el gimnasio?
When are you at the gym?

Phrases with "When"

The underlined verb can be conjugated to match any subject.

... cuando <u>tengo</u> tiempo.   ... when I have time.

Nota Cultural

El Zócalo

The main square in a Mexican town is known as a zócalo. The word in Spanish means "pedestal" or "stand." A zócalo is an open urban space that is a city square. In a zócalo it is common to see trees, fountains and bandstands.

The most famous zócalo in Mexico is the one in Mexico City. It is formally known as La Plaza de la Constitución and was built to commemorate Mexico's independence. This area marks the government district of Mexico City.

Ejercicios

Exercise 1.3a:

Directions: Write the action for the picture.

1.

2.

3.

4.

5.

6.

7.

8.

9.

10.

1. _____
   _____

2. _____
   _____

3. _____
   _____

4. _____
   _____

5. _____
   _____

6. _____
   _____

7. _____
   _____

8. _____
   _____

9. _____
   _____

10. _____
    _____

Ejercicios

Exercise 1.3b:

Directions: Match the place to the action.

1. ____ el centro comercial	a. trabajar
3. ____ el parque	b. pasar tiempo con amigos
4. ____ la escuela	c. comprar cosas
5. ____ el gimnasio	d. ir de compras
6. ____ la biblioteca	e. ver una exposición
7. ____ la iglesia	f. comer y beber
8. ____ el trabajo	g. bajar información
9. ____ el hotel	h. rezar
10. ____ el hospital	i. estudiar y aprender
11. ____ el banco	j. nadar
12. ____ la tienda	k. ahorrar dinero
13. ____ el museo	l. tener un examen médico
14. ____ el restaurante	m. hacer noche
15. ____ la plaza	n. hacer ejercicios
16. ____ la piscina	o. caminar con el perro

Exercise 1.3c:

Directions: Write a sentence that states what the person/people does/do at each location. Make sure you conjugate the verbs correctly. Follow the example.

Example: Juan está en el banco.   <u>Juan ahorra el dinero.</u>

1. Yo estoy en la biblioteca.   _____

2. Elena está en el trabajo.   _____

3. Nosotros estamos en el restaurante.   _____

4. Ellos están en la sinagoga.   _____

5. Mi madre está en el parque.   _____

6. Tú estás en el hospital.   _____

7. Mi padre está en el correo.   _____

8. Uds. están en el museo.   _____

9. Vosotros estáis en el hotel.   _____

10. Yo estoy en la piscina.   _____

Ejercicios

Exercise 1.3d:

Directions: Reorder the sentences to make them correct. Use the example as a guide.
Example: trabajo el estoy en trabajo cuando   Cuando estoy en el trabajo, trabajo.

1. en el parque con el perro cuando estamos caminamos
   _____

2. el correo en envían por están correo cuando
   _____

3. presto muchos estoy en biblioteca libros la cuando
   _____

4. compras cuando está gusta el en comercial le ir de Rebela centro
   _____

5. gusta rezar me en una mezquita cuando estoy
   _____

Exercise 1.3e:

Directions: You want to interview a new neighbor to find out when he/she does things: work, hang out with friends, study, and exercise. Create the questions below.

1. _____

2. _____

3. _____

4. _____

Exercise 1.3f:

Directions: Read the passage and then answer the questions.

Mis amigos están en la plaza porque quieren pasar tiempo allí. Ellos comen y beben en un restaurante al lado de la plaza. Después, ellos caminan a la biblioteca. Están en la biblioteca porque necesitan navegar en Internet para bajar información y prestar libros. Luego, quieren ir de compras en las tiendas en el centro comercial. Ellos compran ropa y cosas para la escuela. Por fin, ellos van a casa para descansar.

Answer Cierto (True) or Falso (False).
1.   ___ The restaurant is in the "plaza."
2.   ___ They go to the mall after they eat.
3.   ___ At the mall, they do not shop.
4.   ___ It appears they are researching at the library.
5.   ___ The day is spent with friends.

SECTION 1.4 - GOING PLACES

■ DAY 1

OBJECTIVES

You will learn:
- To state where people go

Going Places

In this section, you will be able to talk about where you are going. With a little instruction, you will learn to combine the vocabulary learned for places in your town or city with the verb in Spanish "to go." In doing this, you will be able to express your destination and the destination of your friends.

To Go

Below is the verb conjugation for the verb "ir" in Spanish. This present tense conjugation is used when you want to express any form of "go" or "going."

Ir- To Go

Yo	voy	I go, I am going	Nosotros Nosotras	vamos	We go, we are going
Tú	vas	You go, you are going	Vosotros Vosotras	vais	All of you go, all of you are going
Él Ella Usted (Ud.)	va	He goes, he is going She goes, she is going You (formal) go, you (formal) are going	Ellos Ellas Ustedes (Uds.)	van	They go, they are going All of you go, all of you are going

Sentence Formation

To state where you or someone else is going, you will use the conjugated form of the verb "ir." Then, you will need to follow the verb with the word "a" which means "to."
Finally you will state the place where you or someone else is going.

Yo voy a la plaza.   I am going to the plaza.

Antonio va a la piscina hoy.   Antonio goes to the pool today.

A + el

In instances when the place of destination is masculine, you would have the definite article "el" preceded by the word "a." When this happens, a contraction occurs where the "a" and the "el" combine to form "al." If you remember, this is similar to the contraction "del" that occurs when the "de" and "el" are next to each other in a sentence.

> Incorrect: Yo voy **a el** cine.
> Correct: Yo voy **al** cine.
> Meaning: I am going to the movie theater.

Examples:

Nosotros vamos al parque este fin de semana.	We are going to the park this weekend.
Ellos van a la escuela todos los días.	They go to school everyday.
Vas al restaurante con tu novio.	You're going to the restaurant with your boyfriend.

■ Day 2

OBJECTIVES

You will learn to:
- To ask and answer where going
- To say and ask location, do, and go

▌ To Ask Where Someone Is Going ▐

To ask where someone is going, you follow the pattern below.

> ¿Adónde vas (tú)*?   To where are you going?

*Word in parentheses is optional.

You can easily change the subject and verb of the sentence to ask where others are going. It is essential, though, that the question word remains "¿adónde?" and not "¿dónde?" The preposition "to," in Spanish "a," needs to have a place in the sentence.

Examples:

¿Adónde va?	To where is he/she going?
¿Adónde van?	To where are they going?
¿Adónde vais?	To where are all of you going?

Nota Cultural

Los Continentes en Español

When you want to say where a country is located or to where you are going, you may want to use the name of the continents in Spanish.

Here is a list:

África
Antártica
Asia
Australia
Europa
Norteamérica
Sudamérica

Can you label the map correctly with these terms?

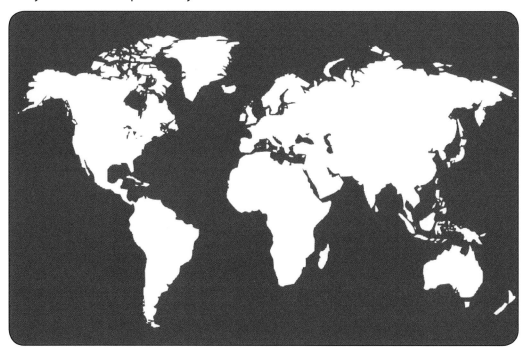

Ejercicios

Exercise 1.4a:

Directions: Give the subject of the sentence.

1. _____ no vais al hospital porque no tenéis tiempo.
2. _____ voy a la tienda para ir de compras.
3. _____ van al concierto esta noche.
4. _____ vamos a la fiesta con nuestros amigos.
5. _____ va a la casa de su novio (boyfriend).
6. _____ no vas hoy porque estás enfermo.
7. ¡_____ no voy!
8. _____ va al supermercado con su madre.

Exercise 1.4b:

Directions: Based on the picture and subject, make a sentence in Spanish stating where the person/people are going.

1.

2.

3.

4.

5.

1. Tú y yo   _____
2. Migueleña y Graciela   _____
3. José   _____
4. Tú   _____
5. Yo   _____

Ejercicios

Exercise 1.4c:

Directions: Choose the correct word or word combination from the word bank to correctly complete the sentence. Some words or word combinations may be used more than once or not at all.

Word Bank

al   a la   del   de la   nothing

1. Ana va _____ correo para comprar sellos.
2. Ana está cerca _____ correo.
3. Ana está en _____ el correo.
4. Beto está en _____ la piscina.
5. Beto va _____ piscina.
6. Beto está detrás _____ piscina.

Exercise 1.4d:

Directions: Ask where the following people are going.

1. Bernardo   _____
2. Mónica y tú   _____
3. Ellos   _____
4. Tú   _____
5. Uds.   _____

Ejercicios

Exercise 1.4e:

Directions: Answer the questions based on the information.

Elide→ banco
Manolo→ escuela
Xav y tú→ parque
Emilio y Eric→ gimnasio
Tú→ hotel

¿Adónde va Elide?   _____
¿Adónde va Manolo?   _____
¿Adónde vais Xav y tú?   _____
¿Adónde van Emilio y Eric?   _____
¿Adónde vas tú?   _____

Exercise 1.4f:

Directions: Answer the questions in a full sentence in Spanish about where you and your friends and family typically go.

1. ¿Adónde van tú y tu familia para comer?_____

2. ¿Adónde vas tú para hacer ejercicio? _____

3. ¿Adónde vas tú después de la escuela? _____

4. ¿Adónde van tus amigos para pasar tiempo? _____

SECTION 1.5 - SPECIALTY STORES

■ DAY 1

OBJECTIVES

You will learn:

- To list names of stores
- To recognize and form the pattern for store name formation

Specialty Stores

In Spanish it is easy to figure out what items specialty stores sell. The actual word in Spanish for the item sold at the store is in the store name. To form the rest of the word, the suffix "-ería" is used to indicate where something is made, sold, or repaired.

Let's look at a list of items sold and their store names.

Item	Meaning	Store
La carne	The meat	La carnicería
La flor	The flower	La florería
La fruta	The fruit	La frutería
El helado	The ice cream	La heladería
La joya	The jewel	La joyería
El juego/el juguete	The game/toy	La juguetería
El libro	The book	La librería
El pan	The bread	La panadería
El papel	The paper	La papelería
El zapato	The shoe	La zapatería

Take a look at these examples, and notice that the noun + "ería" pattern varies slightly in some cases:

1. The last vowel on the end of the noun of the item is dropped and the suffix "-ería" is added.

   Ejemplo: fruta drops "a" → frutería

2. Sometimes the last vowel is not dropped and a consonant is added to the word.

   Ejemplo: carne → carnicería

Examples:

Here of some examples of how this vocabulary looks in questions are sentences.

¿Dónde está la zapatería?	Where is the shoe store?
La zapatería está al lado de la papelería.	The shoe store is next to the paper store.
¿Adónde vas?	Where are you going?
Yo voy a la librería.	I am going to the bookstore.

■ DAY 2

OBJECTIVES

You will learn to:

- To state for what reason people go to stores
- To ask for what reason people go to stores
- To say where to buy things
- To list additional reasons to go to specialty stores

Para

If you want to say for what reason you are going to a place, you use the word in "para" in Spanish. "Para" means "for," "in order to," or "to." The word "para" in Spanish is followed by an infinitive. The examples show provide a clear understanding of how "para" is used in a sentence.

Yo voy al parque para caminar con el perro.	I am going to the park to walk the dog.
Para comprar sellos, yo necesito ir al correo.	In order to buy stamps, I need to go to the post office.
Juan va a la biblioteca para los libros.	Juan goes to the library for books.

¿Para qué?

When you want to ask for what reason someone is going to a place, you also use the word "para." A question with "para qué" can typically translate to mean "why." The format of the question is in the examples below.

¿Para qué vas al supermercado?	Why (for what reason) are you going to the supermarket?
Voy para comprar la leche.	I am going to buy milk.
¿Para qué razón van a la universidad?	Why (for what reason) are they going to the university?
Van para estudiar fotografía.	They're going to study photography.

Reasons to go

Here are a couple of additional vocabulary words that provide reasons to go to places.

Buscar	to look for
Conocer a nuevos amigos	to meet new friends
Encontrar	to find
Hacer fotocopias	to make photocopies
Pagar (por)	to pay (for)
Tomar helado	to eat ice cream
Vender	to sell

Nota Cultural

Alternatives to Specialty Stores

Super-stores

In all Spanish speaking countries, it is common to buy specific items at specialty stores. However, these stores are NOT the only places to buy specific items. Often times, immediately outside urban areas, you will be able to find massive stores that have a wide variety of goods and services. Here is a list of some of these stores in Mexico. In each country, there will be stores of this same type, but under different ownership.

Aurrera
Bodega Comerical Mexicana
Bodega Gigante
Carrefour
Gigante
Wal-mart

Street Vendors

Another alternative to specialty stores are street vendors. Street vendors would be on the opposite end to super-stores. Street vendors are not associated with large corporations. Typically street vendors produce and sell their own goods. For example, someone with a farm or land may be a fruit and vegetable vendor. Another person who is a good cook may make tortillas, breads, or pastries. Street vendors may sell their goods on the side of the road or at a local market.

Ejercicios

Exercise 1.5a:

Directions: Match the item to its specialty store. This is new vocabulary.

1. ____El dulce	(the sweet)	a. La verdulería
2. ____La gasolina	(the gas)	b. La pastelería
3. ____El pescado	(the fish)	c. La pescadería
4. ____La verdura	(the vegetable)	d. La dulcería
5. ____El pastel	(the pastry)	e. La gasolinera

Exercise 1.5b:

Directions: Based on what you need, tell to what specialty store you are going.

1. Tú necesitas comprar las flores.   _____

2. Tú necesitas comprar mucho pan.   _____

3. Tú necesitas comprar las frutas.   _____

4. Tú necesitas comprar libros.   _____

5. Tú necesitas comprar las joyas.   _____

Exercise 1.5c:

Directions: Label the stores according to their specialty store name.

_____   _____   _____

_____   _____

Ejercicios

Exercise 1.5d:

Give the reason in a full sentence in Spanish why you are going to the store in the picture.

1. _____

2. _____

3. _____

4. _____

5. _____

Exercise 1.5e:

En una verdulería, se venden las verduras.
In a vegetable store, vegetables are sold.

1. En una frutería, se venden _____.

2. En una pescadería, se venden _____.

3. En una dulcería, se venden _____.

4. En una gasolinera, se venden _____.

5. En una pastelería, se venden _____.

6. En una florería, se venden _____.

7. En una librería, se venden _____.

8. En una juguetería, se venden _____.

Ejercicios

Exercise 1.5f:

Directions: Make an advertisement for your own specialty store. Follow the model. Make sure to include: the name, the phone number, the hours and days of operation, the services provided.

Papelería Ramos
011 52 725 9628
lunes a vienes
de 09:00 a 19:00

Nuestros Servicios

Vender Papel de
gran calidad para
la impresión

Vender productos
empresarios:
Cartulinas
Carpetas
Sobres

Hacer servicios
fotocopiados

NOTES

Section 1.1 _____ Date

Section 1.2 _____ Date

Section 1.3 _____ Date

Section 1.4 _____ Date

_____
_____
_____
_____
_____
_____
_____
_____
_____
_____

Section 1.5 _____ Date

_____
_____
_____
_____
_____
_____
_____
_____
_____
_____
_____

Additional Notes _____ Date

_____
_____
_____
_____
_____
_____
_____
_____
_____
_____
_____

SECTION 1.6 - FUTURE PLANS

■ DAY 1

OBJECTIVES

You will learn:
- To use the simple future
- To ask where self and others are going to go

Future Plans

When you want to say where you or others are going later on today or in the near future, you use the verb "ir." Sentences such as, "I am going to go to the park later," or "tomorrow they are going to the store to buy clothes for school" are all examples of the near future. In today's lesson you will learn to use this pattern in Spanish.

Going To...

To form sentences that express the near future, you need to do three simple things.

1. Use a conjugated form of the verb "ir" in present tense.
2. Follow the conjugated form of the verb "ir" with the word "a."
3. Finally, add the infinitive that states the action the will occur in the near future.

    Let's look at the pattern and some examples.

Pattern

(Subject)* + **conjugated form of "ir"** + **a** + **infinitive** + remainder of sentence.

*Subjects in parentheses are optional.

Examples

(Yo) +**voy a** + **jugar** + **al tenis** en el parque más tarde.
I am going to play tennis in the park later.

Vamos a ir al cine mañana par ver una película nueva.
We are going to go the movie theater tomorrow to see a new movie.

Juan no puede ir. **Va a hacer** la tarea en vez de pasar tiempo con nosotros.
Juan can't go. He's going to do home work instead of hanging out with us.

| Asking Questions |

When you want to ask when someone is going to do something, you use the same pattern, only with an interrogative word. Let's look at some examples:

¿Cuándo vas a visitar a tu familia?
When are you going to visit your family?

¿Adónde van a ir?
Where are they going to go?

¿Por qué va a estar en Miami Shakira?
Why is Shakira going to be in Miami?

¿Para qué razón vamos a ir al parque?
Why are we going to go to the park?

¿Quién va a practicar deportes?
Who is going to practice sports?

■ DAY 2

OBJECTIVES

You will learn to:

- To talk about going places on certain days of the week
- To express: "Let's go _____!"

| On + Days of the Week |

To talk about doing something on certain day/s of the week, you need to put the words "el" or "los" in front of the day/s.

If you would "el" in front of the day of the week, it would mean that you are going to do something only on that specific day.

Pattern: El lunes – on Monday
                El lunes voy a la piscina. -On Monday I'm going to the pool.

If you place "los" in front of the day/s of the week, it means that you do something on those consecutive days of the week.

Pattern: Los lunes- on Mondays

                  Los lunes voy a la piscina. – On Mondays (in general) I go to the pool.

Review of the Days of the Week

Look at the list below to review the days of the week. Remember that the days of the week are not capitalized except when they begin a sentence or are part of a title.

lunes- Monday
martes – Tuesday
miércoles- Wednesday
jueves- Thursday
viernes- Friday
sábado- Saturday
domingo- Sunday

Examples

El viernes voy a jugar al golf con mi padre.
On Friday I am going to play golf with my father.

Los viernes juego al golf con mi padre.
On Fridays I play golf with my father.

Los domingos mi familia y yo vamos a la iglesia Holy Name.
On Sundays my family and I go to Holy Name church.

El jueves tengo un examen médico.
On Thursday I have a check-up.

Nota Cultural

Let's Go!

Use "¡Vamos!" when you want to tell someone, "let's go!"

        ¡Vamos, Claudia!
        ¡Vamos, Ernesto!

Exercises

Exercise 1.6a:

Directions: Pick out the pattern to form the simple future:
                    by underlining the conjugated form of "ir,"
                    by circling the letter "a," and
                    by blocking the infinitive.
          Then, write the meaning of the sentence.

1. Voy a ir de compras en el mercado esta tarde.
   Meaning: _____

2. Las señoras van a hacer ejercicio en el gimnasio esta noche después de trabajar.
   Meaning: _____

3. Voy a ir a tomar helado con mi primo a la heladería que está al lado del parque.
   Meaning: _____

4. ¿Vamos a caminar con nuestro perro nuestro mañana por la mañana?
   Meaning: _____

5. Ricardo va a bajar información en la biblioteca.
   Meaning: _____

Exercise 1.6b:

Directions: Based on your schedule, write sentences about what you are going to be doing today.

Fecha: 10 de marzo

09:00- Gimnasio
10:00- Escuela
11:00- Pollo Frito
        Kentucky
12:00- Plaza
13:00- Escuela
14:00- Casa

1. Primero, _____

2. Después, _____

3. Luego, _____

4. Al mediodía, _____

5. Después, _____

6. Por fin, _____

Exercise 1.6c:

Directions: Answer Cierto (True) or Falso (False) based on the information contained in the statement.

1. _____ Ellos van a enviar cartas en la piscina.
2. _____ Vamos a rezar en el templo.
3. _____ Voy a correr y levantar pesos en el banco.
4. _____ Carlos va a vender ropa en su trabajo en el centro comercial.
5. _____ Van a prestar unos libros en la librería.

The answers to the next exercises will be based on the calendar.

HORARIO DE RONALDO

LUNES	MARTES	MIERCOLES	JUEVES	VIERNES	SABADO	DOMINGO
		1	2	3 examen médico	4	5 templo
6 lección de piano	7 béisbol	8	9 béisbol	10	11 concierto de Marc Anthony	12 templo
13 lección de piano	14 béisbol	15	16 béisbol	17	18	19 templo
20 lección de piano	21 béisbol	22	23 béisbol	24	25 concierto de Chayanne	26 templo
27 lección de piano	28 béisbol	29 fiesta de cumpleaños	30 béisbol	31		

Exercise 1.6d:

Directions: Write Cierto (True) or Falso (False).

1. _____ Los miércoles, Ronaldo tiene una fiesta.
2. _____ El martes y el jueves, Ronaldo va a jugar al béisbol.
3. _____ Los domingos, Ronaldo va al templo.
4. _____ Ronaldo toca el piano los lunes.

Exercises

Exercise 1.6e:

Directions: Answer the questions in a full sentence in Spanish.

1. ¿En qué días tiene las lecciones de piano Ronaldo?

_____

2. ¿En qué días va al templo Ronaldo?

_____

3. ¿En qué días va a los conciertos Ronaldo?

_____

4. ¿En qué días normalmente no hace nada Ronaldo?

_____

5. ¿En qué día tiene un examen médico Ronaldo?

_____

Exercise 1.6f:

Directions: Answer the questions with Sí (Yes) or No (No).

1. Can you use "en" to mean "on" for days of the week? _____

2. Can you use "el" or "los" to mean "on" for days of the week? _____

3. Does "el martes" mean "on Tuesday"? _____

4. Does "los martes" mean "on Tuesdays"? _____

5. Are the days of the week capitalized normally? _____

6. To review the formation of the date, do you normally structure it, "el + day + de + month" (example: el 15 de noviembre)? _____

SECTION 1.7 - INVITING SOMEONE

■ DAY 1

OBJECTIVES

You will learn to:

- To invite someone somewhere
- To state that someone is coming with you

Inviting Someone

When you want to invite someone somewhere, you can say it a couple of ways. The first way would be one that you already know by using the verb "querer." The infinitive of any verb can follow the conjugated form of "querer." You can use any form of the conjugated verb "querer."

Let's first review the conjugations of "querer" in present tense:

Querer- To Want

Yo	quiero	= I want	Nosotros Nosotras	queremos= We want
Tú	quieres	= You want	Vosotros Vosotras	queréis = All of you want
Él Ella Usted (Ud.)	quiere	= He wants = She wants = You (formal) want	Ellos Ellas Ustedes (Uds.)	quieren = They want = All of you want

¿Quieres ir conmigo?   Do you want to go with me?

¿Quieres acompañarme al concierto? Do you want to accompany me to the concert?

Another way to ask someone is by using a couple of phrases that come from the verb "invitar." Place the word "a" after "invitar," then add an infinitive.

| Te invito a ir conmigo. | I invite you to go with me. |
| Te invito a cenar. | I am inviting you to dinner. |

Yet another way to invite someone to go somewhere is by using the verb "venir." You can use it in the infinitive form after a verb, or you can conjugate and use it alone.

¿Quieres venir a mi casa?	Do you want to come to my house?
¿Vas a venir?	Are you going to come?
¿Vienes conmigo?	Are you coming with me?

Venir

The conjugation of the verb "venir" is below. The verb "venir" is called a "-go" verb because of the changes in its conjuction in the "yo" form, vengo. You will also notice that this is a stem-changing verb; you will learn more about stem-changing verbs in the future. For now, a stem changing verb is a verb that has a change in its stem, or root. With the verb "venir," the "e" changes to "ie" in all forms except for "nosotros" and "vosotros."

**Venir - to come
(e-ie)**

Yo vengo = I come/am coming	Nosotros venimos= We come/are coming Nosotras
Tú vienes = You come/are coming	Vosotros venís= All of you come/ Vosotras are coming

Él   viene   = He comes/is coming
Ella   = She comes/is coming
Usted (Ud.)   = You (formal) comes/are
                         coming
	Ellos vienen= They come/ are coming
	Ellas
	Ustedes (Uds.) = All of you come/ are
	                         coming

■ DAY 2

OBJECTIVES

You will learn to:

- To state and ask when someone is coming versus going

- To demonstrate an understanding of the differences between come and go

- To demonstrate an understanding of "te invito"

Ir versus Venir

Sometimes it is difficult for native speakers of English to differentiate between the verbs in Spanish "ir" and "venir." The goal of this lesson is to clarify the meanings of "ir" and "venir" so that there will be no confusion for an English speaker learning Spanish.

While "ir" means "to go" and "venir" means "to come" the use of the two can be confusing. Although there is some flexibility in English to interchange the verbs, in Spanish it is not the case. Here are some examples of how the verbs can be somewhat interchangeable.

Are you coming with me?

Are you going with me?

Above the two sentences in English mean roughly the same thing, but is Spanish the same sentences would have different meanings.

Before you receive examples of the differences in Spanish between "ir" and "venir," it is important to understand the uses of each.

-"Ir" always refers to someone or something moving away from the speaker.

-"Venir" always refers to someone or something moving towards the speaker.

Examples:

Vas al supermercado.
You are going to the supermarket.
(speaker is not at the supermarket; person who is going to the supermarket is moving away from the location of the speaker.)

Vienes para visitarme en casa.
You are coming to visit me.
(speaker is home; person who is coming to visit moves towards the speaker's home.)

 Nota Cultural

"Te invito."

The phrase "te invito" is a way of inviting someone to go somewhere or do something. But, there is an additional meaning to the invitation. When someone uses this phrase to invite you some place or include you, it means that they are also treating you to that activity.

To understand what "te invito" means, read the follow scenario and it's translation.

Persona A: ¿Quieres ir a tomar un café conmigo esta tarde? Te invito.

Persona B: Claro, pero solamente si me permites invitarte mañana.

Persona A: Do you want to get coffee with me this afternoon. It's my treat.

Persona B: Sure, but only if you allow me to treat you tomorrow.

Person A not only invited Person B out for coffee, but it is the intention of Person A to pay for Person B's coffee.

Person B understands this and wants to return the favor by buying Person A coffee tomorrow.

Exercises 1.7a:

Directions: Fill in the appropriate conjugated form of the verb "venir."

1. Yo _____ a la fiesta.
2. Quieres _____ al baile, ¿no?
3. Verónica y Melina _____ a la biblioteca para estudiar a las 6.
4. Vosotros _____ cuando tenéis tiempo.
5. ¿_____ tú con mi hermana?
6. Leonardo no _____ porque tiene que trabajar.

Exercise 1.7b:

Directions: Based on the scenario, ask the people to come with you.

1. Invite your friend to come with you to the mall _____

2. Ask a relative if he go to come to dinner   _____

3. Invite your boyfriend/girlfriend to the movies   _____

4. Ask if your friend is coming with you   _____

Exercise 1.7c:
Directions: Write a response to the following invitations.

1. ¿Quieres ir conmigo?   _____

2. Te invito a tomar un café.   _____

3. ¿Quieres venir a mi casa?   _____

4. ¿Vienes conmigo a visitar a mi familia? _____

Exercise 1.7d:

Directions: Explain in English the meaning of the sentences.

1. Miguel va a la escuela.

2. Miguel viene a la escuela.

Exercises

Exercise 1.7e:

Directions: Circle whether the people are moving toward or away from speaker.

1. Toward   Away   Juan y yo venimos a visitar.
2. Toward   Away   Miranda viene pronto.
3. Toward   Away   Quieren venir conmigo.
4. Toward   Away   Quieren ir a la heladería.
5. Toward   Away   Tú vienes a la fiesta.

Exercise 1.7f:

Directions: Pretend you are writing an email to invite your friend to eat with you. Make sure the friend know that you are treating him/her.

To:
From:
Subject:

Querido/a _____,

                                         Hasta pronto, _____

SECTION 1.8 - SALIR

■ DAY 1

You will learn:

- To state why people leave an event
- To ask if people are leaving an event

Salir

When you want to say that you are leaving a place, you can use the verb "salir." The verb "salir" has a couple of meanings, but when "salir" is followed by the preposition "de" it means to leave from a place.

"Salir" follows the same conjugation pattern as "venir." It is conjugated using the -ir verb pattern, except in the first person. It is also known as a "-go" verb because of its irregular conjugation in the first person.

Salir - to leave (a place)

Yo salgo ...- I leave, am leaving	Nosotros salimos...- We leave/are Nosotras leaving
Tú sales ...- You leave, are leaving	Vosotros salís ...- All of you leave/ Vosotras are leaving

Él   sale ...- He leaves, is leaving
Ella   She leaves, is leaving
Usted (Ud.)   You (formal) leave, are
                          leaving
	Ellos salen ...- They leave/ are
	Ellas leaving
	Ustedes (Uds.) All of you leave/
	                          are leaving

Examples

Catalina sale de la casa.	Catalina leaves the house.
Salimos de la fiesta a las 9.	We are leaving the party at 9.
Quieres salir en una hora.	You want to leave in an hour.

Other Expressions with "Salir"

If you want to use "salir" without the expression "de" it simply means "to go out" or "to leave." When you add "con" after the word "salir," it means "to go out on a date with someone."

Yo salgo por las noches.	I go out at night.
Gabriel sale con Yolanda.	Gabriel dates Yolanda.

■ Day 2

OBJECTIVES

You will learn to:

- To state that you and others are returning from a place
- To ask when others are returning from an event

Returning from a Place

Naturally, when you go some place, you eventually return. There are a couple of ways to say "to return" in Spanish, but only two forms would be appropriate when you talk about people returning from places. They are the infinitives "regresar" and "volver." Both are used with the preposition "de" after them to signify the place of return.

In this section, you will see the conjugations of both "regresar" and "volver." The examples will show you how both can be synonymous to mean "return." It is important to learn both ways to express "return" because some countries prefer the use of one verb to the other.

Regresar

The verb "regresar" is conjugated as a regular -ar verb in the present tense.

Regresar- to return

Yo regreso – I return/am returning	Nosotros regresamos- We return/are returning Nosotras
Tú regresas - You return/are returning	Vosotros regresáis - All of you return/ Vosotras are returning
Él regresa - He returns/ is returning Ella She returns/is returning Usted (Ud.) You (formal) return/are returning	Ellos regresan - They return/are returning Ellas returning Ustedes (Uds.) All of you return/ are returning

Volver and Stem Changing Verbs

The verb "volver" is a stem changing verb. This is because the stem, or root, of the verb has spelling changing in four of the six conjugations. There are many stem changing verbs in Spanish.

Stem changing verbs fall into one of three categories. To know what category a stem changing verbs belongs, you look at the vowel in the stem, or root, of the infinitive. The three categories of stem changing verbs are the following:

o → ue
e → ie
e → i

The verb "volver" fits into the first category. There is a list of some other common verbs that fit into this category as well. You will learn more about the other two categories of stem changing verbs in another unit.

o → ue

Contar	to count
Costar	to cost
Soñar	to dream
Dormir	to sleep
Encontrar	to find
Morir	to die
Mover	to move
Poder	to be able to, can
Recordar	to remember

The changes to the verb "volver" not only occur in the stem, or root, but the verb must also be conjugated in the present tense to match the subject. You will notice that when the changes occur in the stem, they do NOT occur for the "-emos" and "éis" conjugations. This is true for all stem changing verbs. Because of this, stem changing verbs can also be known as "shoe verbs" because the chart can resemble a sneaker or boot.

Volver- To Return

Yo vuelvo – I return/am returning	Nosotros volvemos- We return/are Nosotras returning
Tú vuelves- You return/are returning	Vosotros volvéis- All of you return/ Vosotras are returning

Él   vuelve- He returns/ is returning
 Ella   She returns/is returning
 Usted (Ud.)   You (formal) return/are
                    returning
	Ellos vuelven- They return/ are
	 Ellas returning
	 Ustedes (Uds.) All of you return/ are
	                    returning

Examples

Ellos regresan de las vacaciones hoy.	They are returning from vacation today.
Ellos vuelven de las vacaciones hoy.	They are returning from vacation today.
Yo regreso de Colombia en una semana.	I return from Colombia in a week.
Yo vuelvo de Colombia en una semana.	I return from Colombia in a week.

Nota Cultural

"Volver"

Did you know that in 2006, Pedro Almodóvar released his movie "Volver" to the public? Penélope Cruz, a famous Spanish and American actor, is the lead in this movie.

The movie is about the mother of two sisters who returns from "the dead" to help them find resolution to some of life's problems.

The movie received wonderful reviews.   If you can, see if you can rent it!

Exercises

Exercises 1.8a:

Directions: Read the conversation and then summarize.

Sofía: Oye, Adela. ¿Cómo estás?
Adela: Bien. ¿Adónde vas?
Sofía: Voy a la biblioteca para estudiar.
Adela: ¡Qué bueno! Voy también. ¿Quieres venir conmigo?
Sofía: Tal vez vengo. ¿A qué hora vas?
Adela: Voy en 5 minutos después de salir de aquí.
Sofía: Bueno, salimos juntas.
Adela: Excelente.

Summary: _____

_____

_____

Exercise 1.8b:

Directions: Fill in correct form of the conjugated verb "salir."

1. Ellos _____ del gimnasio muy pronto.
2. Yo _____ con mi novio.
3. Nosotros _____ de nuestra casa en una hora.
4. Juanita _____ con Jorge.
5. Uds. _____ del museo cuando se cierra.

Exercise 1.8c:

Directions: Create a comic strip. Make sure to ask and answer questions that include in Spanish the verbs: to go, to come, to leave.

Exercises

Exercise 1.8d:

Directions: Conjugate the stem changing verbs correctly.

1. La ropa _____ mucho dinero.
2. Yo _____ de Europa en abril.
3. En 2 idiomas, el español y el ingles, tú _____ con los números de 0 a 199.
4. Ellos _____ de las vacaciones en un día.
5. Cuando duermo, nunca _____ .

Exercise 1.8e:

Directions: Based on the information, write a sentence saying from where the people return.

1. Mi padre, Store _____

2. Mi madre, Supermarket _____

3. Mi hermano, School _____

4. Mi hermana, Pool _____

Exercise 1.8f:

Directions: Match the forms of the verb and their meaning.

1. ___, ___ He returns   a. regreso   g. vuelves
2. ___, ___ They return   b. regresan   h. vuelven
3. ___, ___ All of you return   c. vuelvo   i. regresáis
4. ___, ___ You return   d. volvéis   j. vuelve
5. ___, ___ I return   e. regresamos   k. regresa
6. ___, ___ We return   f. regresas   l. volvemos

SECTION 1.9 - GOING PLACES

■ DAY 1

OBJECTIVES

You will learn:

- To list phrases on the topic of making plans

- To make plans

- To ask and answer questions about making plans

Making Plans Part I

In this unit, you already learned so much about getting around your town or city. These final two lessons will prepare you to make plans with people so that you can go and enjoy the places in your town or city.

Making Plans

¿Te gustaría ir a....	Would you like to go...?
Ya tengo planes.	I already have plans.
Tengo una cita.	I have a date.
(No) puedo ir.	I can (not) go.
Lo siento, pero....	I am sorry, but....
Tal vez	maybe/perhaps
Me gustaría....	I would like to....
Claro que sí.	Of course.
Te invito a....	I invite you to....
Hoy no, tal vez otro día.	Not today, maybe another day.
Ya voy.	I am already going.
No sé si....	I don't know if....

Examples of Usage

The following dialogue is meant to provide appropriate ways to use the vocabulary that will allow you to make plans. Although the situation is informal, you can use this vocabulary in a more formal way. In fact, you can and should manipulate this vocabulary for your comfort and for each situation.

Diálogo

Persona A: Oye, Juan. ¿Qué vas a hacer mañana?
Persona B: No sé. ¿Por qué?
Persona A: Mi novia y yo tenemos una cita. Y, ella tiene una amiga...
Persona B: ¿Quieres saber si me gustaría acompañarles
en su cita con la amiga de tu novia?
Persona A: Bueno, supongo que sí.
Persona B: ¿Es simpática la chica?
Persona A: Muy simpática. Y, tienes la clase de español con la chica. Es Elena.
Persona B: Elena es fantástica. Puedo ir. ¿Adónde van y a qué hora?

Persona A: Al restaurante Guiguí a las 8.
Persona B: Lo siento, pero necesito regresar temprano. Tengo planes a las 10.
Persona A: No pasa nada. No hay ningún problema.
Persona B: Me voy. Hasta mañana.

Translation of Dialogue

Persona A: Hey, Juan. What are you doing tomorrow?
Persona B: I don't know. Why?
Persona A: My girlfriend and I have a date. And, she has a friend....
Persona B: You want to know if I would go with you on your date with your girlfriend's friend?
Persona A: Well, I suppose so.
Persona B: Is the girl nice?
Persona A: Very nice. And, you have Spanish class with the girl. It's Elena.
Persona B: Elena is fantastic. I can go. Where and what time?
Persona A: Guiguí's restaurant at 8.
Persona B: I am sorry, but I have to leave early. I have plans at 10.
Persona A: No problem.
Persona B: I'm going. See you tomorrow.

■ DAY 2

OBJECTIVES

You will learn to:

- To list phrases on the topic of making plans
- To make plans
- To ask and answer questions about making plans

Making Plans Part II

There are some additional phrases that will help you in a situation where plans are made. The vocabulary in this lesson is used with the verb "estar" because the vocabulary tells the person's temporary state of being. In addition, because the vocabulary describes the subject, it must modify the subject by matching it in number (singular or plural) and gender (male or female).

Making Plans

Cansado	Tired
Contento	Happy
Enfermo	Ill/sick
Listo	Ready
Ocupado	Busy
Triste	Sad

Examples:

This set of examples demonstrates how the vocabulary words above need to match the subject in number and gender. "Estar" is also conjugated to match the subject.

Adán está ocupado.	Adán is busy.
Pamela está ocupada.	Pamela is busy.
Ellos están ocupados.	They (males) are busy.
Ellas están ocupadas.	They (females) are busy.

 Nota Cultural

Evening Plans

Whether going out with friends for tapas or a movie, Spaniards often start the evening with "el paseo," a leisurely stroll through the main streets or along "el paseo marítimo" in the coastal resorts.

Exercises

Exercise 1.9a:

Directions: Find the vocabulary in the Word Search.

I am sorry.   I have plans.   I can go.

I have a date.   Maybe another day

U	V	G	X	Q	L	L	M	X	W	K	Y	S	A	K
K	K	D	X	W	K	E	T	T	X	P	X	C	T	M
L	O	S	I	E	N	T	O	E	L	Y	Y	S	I	D
Z	I	Z	U	V	O	I	R	V	A	X	E	M	C	A
S	J	P	U	C	M	Y	P	M	K	N	I	F	A	F
B	V	O	U	G	X	K	O	N	A	V	V	W	N	X
U	T	B	Y	E	E	Q	M	L	C	K	V	V	U	N
C	H	C	X	S	D	M	P	S	R	N	V	K	O	R
A	Í	D	O	R	T	O	Z	E	V	L	A	T	G	O
T	A	A	D	K	G	C	I	Z	A	X	I	G	N	M
T	K	R	V	N	I	A	R	R	B	Z	L	Q	E	V
Z	U	W	E	R	A	A	H	M	W	Z	B	C	T	D
V	V	T	L	P	J	S	M	L	C	B	Z	X	H	Z
W	H	E	Q	M	Z	O	G	Q	X	T	T	B	F	P
N	D	Y	R	L	W	M	D	C	B	S	H	I	V	T

Exercises

Exercise 1.9b:

Directions: Fill in the answers to the Criss-Cross puzzle.

Across

5. I would like to go.

Down

1. Would you like to go?
2. Of course.
3. I don't know.
4. I am already going.

Exeercise 1.9c:

Directions: Read the mini-dialogue, and then answer the questions Cierto (True) or Falso (False).

Hidalgo: Buenas tardes. Te llamo para invitarte a cenar conmigo esta noche.
Carlota: Hidalgo, gracias por invitarme. Lo siento, pero ya tengo planes hoy.
Hidalgo: Entonces, ¿te gustaría ir mañana?
Carlota: Tal vez otro día. Mañana mi familia viene de Miami. Puedo ir el jueves.
Hidalgo: Bueno, también puedo ir el jueves.
Carlota: Muchas gracias, Hidalgo.
Hidalgo: No hay de que. Hasta pronto.
Carlota: Chao.

1. _____ Hidalgo y Carlota are on the phone.
2. _____ Hidalgo invites Carlota out to dinner.
3. _____ Carlota is a very busy person.
4. _____ Hidalgo and Carlota will never go out to dinner.

Exercises

Exercise 1.9d:

Directions: Put the phrases in order to create a dialogue.

a. Bueno. Hasta luego.   _____
b. Hola.   _____
c. Buenos días.   _____
d. No puedo.   _____
e. Tal vez otro día.   _____
f. Porque estoy enfermo.   _____
g. ¿Te gustaría ir al cine?   _____
h. Chao.   _____
i. ¿Por qué?   _____

Exercise 1.9e:

Directions: Write what you would say in Spanish based on the situation.

1. You have a lot of homework and very busy.   _____

2. You are sad because you can't go to the party.   _____

3. You are not feeling well.   _____

4. You are happy because it's a beautiful day.   _____

5. You worked a lot and are tired.   _____

SECTION 1.10 - REVIEW

■ DAY 1

OBJECTIVES

You will learn:

- To recall the first half of Unit I

▌ Review ▌

At the end of each unit you will review the main concepts in lessons 1-9. In addition, you will use lesson 10 to combine the concepts into one cohesive idea. Because each unit has a theme, the content of each lesson belongs with the other lessons of the unit. Lesson 10 provides the opportunity to combine all concepts to practice your proficiency.

The following outline lists the important concepts from each lesson. Go back to each lesson and review these concepts.

You should be able to explain the concept as well as use the concept in sentences and questions.

Spanish Review Outline

I. Lesson 1
    A. Direction Words
    B. Giving and Asking Basic Directions

¿Dónde está la chica?	Where is the girl?
La chica está aquí.	The girl is here.

II. Lesson 2
    A. List Places in City or Town
    B. Give Direction in Relation to another Place
    C. Use of "del" and "de la"

¿Dónde está el parque?	¿Dónde está el parque?
El parque está al lado del cine.	El parque está al lado de la plaza.

III. Lesson 3
    A. List Things to Do
    B. State and Ask What Others Do at Location
    C. State and Ask When

IV. Lesson 4
A. State and Ask "Where going"

Ir - To Go

Yo	voy – I go, I am going	Nosotros Nosotras	vamos - We go, we are going
Tú	vas - You go, you are going	Vosotros Vosotras	vais - All of you go, all of you are going
Él Ella Usted (Ud.)	va - He goes, he is going She goes, she is going You (formal) go, you (formal) are going	Ellos Ellas Ustedes (Uds.)	van - They go, they are going All of you go, all of you are going

B. Use of "al" and "a la"

Yo voy **al** cine.

Yo voy **a la** piscina.

V. Lesson 5
A. List and Form Specialty Stores
B. Ask and state for what reason people go to specialty stores

¿Para qué razón vas a la escuela?

Voy a la escuela para aprender el español.

■ DAY 2

OBJECTIVES

You will learn to:
- Recall the second half of Unit I

Spanish Review Outline

VI. Lesson 6
A. State and ask about simple future
B. Use "ir + a"

Pattern

(Subject)* + **conjugated form of "ir"** + a + **infinitive** + remainder of sentence.

Example

Yo voy a ir al restaurante. - I am going to go to the restaurant.

C. State and ask on what days

Pattern: El lunes - on Monday

Pattern: Los lunes- on Mondays

VII. Lesson 7
A. Inviting Someone Somewhere
B. Venir and "-go" verb patterning

Yo vengo = I come/am coming	Nosotros venimos= We come/are coming Nosotras
Tú vienes = You come/are coming	Vosotros venís = All of you come/ Vosotras are coming

Él   viene = He comes/is coming
Ella   =She comes/is coming
Usted (Ud.)   =You (formal) comes/are
                      coming
	Ellos vienen = They come/ are coming
	Ellas
	Ustedes (Uds.) = All of you come/ are
	                      coming

C. Ir versus Venir

"Ir" always refers to someone or something moving away from the speaker.
"Venir" always refers to someone or something moving towards the speaker.

VIII. Lesson 8
A. Leaving a Place
B. Expressions with Salir

Salir- to leave/to go out
Salir de- to leave (from a place)
Salir con- to go out with someone/ to date

C. Returning to a Place
D. Regresar versus Volver
E. Volver and "o to ue"

Volver- To Return

Yo vuelvo – I return/am returning	Nosotros volvemos - We return/are Nosotras returning
Tú vuelves- You return/are returning	Vosotros volvéis - All of you return/ Vosotras are returning

Él   vuelve - He returns/ is returning
Ella   She returns/is returning
Usted (Ud.)   You (formal) return/are
                    returning
	Ellos vuelven - They return/ are
	Ellas returning
	Ustedes (Uds.) All of you return/ are
	                        returning

F. Stem changers- 3 types

o → ue
e → ie
e → i

IX. Lesson 9
    A. Vocabulary for Making Plans
    B. Making Plans to Go Places

Culture Review Outline

In addition to the Spanish concepts, you also learned culture. Please review the culture concepts in this outline.

You should be able to explain each culture concept.

    I.   **Lesson 1**
             - **Madrid**

    II.   **Lesson 2**
             -**Plaza Mayor and Plazas**

    III.   **Lesson 3**
             -**Plaza de la Constitución and Zócalos**

    IV.   **Lesson 4**
             -**Continents in Spanish**

    V.   **Lesson 5**
             -**Alternatives to Specialty Stores**

    VI.   **Lesson 6**
             -**The phrase: "let's go"**

    VII.   **Lesson 7**
             -**The phrase: "te invito"**

    VIII.   **Lesson 8**
             -**"Volver," the movie**

    IX.   **Lesson 9**
             -**Los paseos**

Exercises

Exercise 1.10a:

Directions: Create a map with 5 places. Tell where the places in the map are located in relation to the other places.

1. _____

2. _____

3._____

4. _____

5. _____

Exercise 1.10b:

Directions: Of those 5 places you chose, tell for what reason you would go to that place.

1. _____

2. _____

3._____

4. _____

5. _____

Exercises

Exercise 1.10 c:

Directions: Make a conversation between Fernando and Julieta to include the following:

- an invitation to go somewhere
- a place
- the location of the place
- expressing "going to go" to the place
- expressing "leaving and returning" from the place
- expressing the phrase "let's go"
- vocabulary for making plans

Fernando: _____

Julieta: _____

Fernando: _____

Julieta: _____

Fernando: _____

Julieta: _____

Fernando: _____

Julieta: _____

Fernando: _____

Julieta: _____

Fernando: _____

Julieta: _____

Fernando: _____

Julieta: _____

Fernando: _____

Julieta: _____

Section 1.6 _____ Date

Section 1.7 _____ Date

Section 1.8 _____ Date

Section 1.9 _____ Date

Section 110 _____ Date

Additional Notes _____ Date

AT SCHOOL

SECTION 2.1 - CLASSES

■ DAY 1

You will learn:

– To list classes at school

▌ Classes ▐

Students enrolled in school have or create a schedule of classes. These classes are taken in order to satisfy requirements for graduation. In this section, you will learn to list these classes.

Classes

Las matemáticas	Mathematics
Las ciencias	Science
Las ciencias sociales	Social Studies
El inglés	English
La educación física	Physical Education
El arte	Art
El coro	Chorus
El español	Spanish
La lectura	Reading
La informática	Computing
La economía doméstica	Home Economics
El salón de estudios	Study Hall
El almuerzo	Lunch

Additional Vocabulary

La clase	The class
La asignatura	The subject
La materia	The subject
El horario	The schedule

▌ Las classes ▐

In Spanish, classes and subject are not capitalized except when they are in a title or begin a sentence.

El inglés es a las 2.	English is at 2.
Tengo la clase de español con mis amigos.	I have Spanish class with my friends.

La clase de…

To say that you have a certain class you need to do the following.

- Remove the definite article (el, la, los, las) from in front of the subject.
- Add "la clase de"

Examples:

Las matemáticas	→	La clase de matemáticas
El español	→	La clase de español
La informática	→	La clase de informática

■ Day 2

You will learn to:
- To list classes at school
- To ask what classes others have and what they study

Talking about Classes

Now that you know the names of the most common classes, you can make sentences about your schedule using the Spanish you already know. In this section, you will be able to state at what time you have these subjects.

In addition, this section will provide you with some vocabulary for specialized classes in the disciplines of math, science, and world languages. The goal for you is to be able to ask and answer questions about a course of study for school.

Sentence Formation

The following patterns will allow you some options for making sentences about your class schedule.

Patterns with "tener"

Form of "tener" + class + "a las"+ time.

"A las" + time + form of "tener" + class.

Examples with "tener"

    Tengo el arte a las 5.   I have Art at 5.

    A las 5 tengo el arte.   At 5 I have Art.

Pattern with "estudiar"

    Form of "estudiar" + class.

Example with "estudiar"

    Estudia el español.   He studies Spanish.

Question Formation

Patterns with "tener"

    ¿Qué + materias + form of "tener"?

    ¿A qué hora + form of "tener" + class?

    ¿Form of "tener" + class?

Examples with "tener"

    ¿Qué materias tienes?   What subjects do you have?

    ¿A qué hora tienes el arte?   At what time do you have Art?

    ¿Tienes el arte?   Do you have Art?

Patterns with "estudiar"

    ¿Qué + materias + form of "estudiar"?

    ¿Form of "estudiar" + class?

Examples with "estudiar"

    ¿Qué materias estudia?   What subjects does he study?

    ¿Estudia el español?   Does he study Spanish?

More Classes

La química	Chemistry
La física	Physics
La biología	Biology
La geometría	Geometry
La trigonometría	Trigonometry
El álgebra	Álgebra
El calculo	Calculus
El latín	Latin
El alemán	German
El francés	French
El chino	Chinese
El italiano	Italian

 Nota Cultural

School in Spain

In Spain, it is the government's responsibility to provide grade school, secondary school, and even higher education. The education is free, but parents typically have to pay for books, supplies, and extra-curricular activities which include arts, crafts, and sports.

Ejercicios

Exercise 2.1a:

Directions: Write the name in Spanish of the class. Follow the example.

Example:    La clase de español

1.

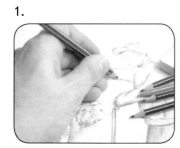

2.

3.

4.

5.

6.

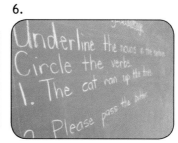

1._____

2._____

3._____

4._____

5._____

6._____

Ejercicios

Exercise 2.1b:

Directions: Based on the schedule, answer the questions Cierto (True) or Falso (Falso).]

Hora	Materias
8:00	Ciencias
9:00	Informática
10:00	Matemáticas
11:00	Inglés
12:00	Español
1:00	Ciencias Sociales

1. ___ Social Studies is at 8:00.
2. ___ Mathematics is before English.
3. ___ The student takes reading.
4. ___ The student takes computing.
5. ___ There is no lunch in this student's schedule.

Exercise 2.1c:

Directions: Match the English to the Spanish.

1. ___ La asignatura   a. class
2. ___ La clase   b. lunch
3. ___ El salón de estudios   c. art
4. ___ El coro   d. schedule
5. ___ La lectura   e. chorus
6. ___ La economía doméstica   f. social studies
7. ___ El horario   g. subject
8. ___ El almuerzo   h. home economics
9. ___ El arte   i. reading
10. ___ Las ciencias sociales   j. study hall

Ejercicios

Exercise 2.1d:

Directions: Circle the most appropriate answer.

1. Si te gustan las ciencias, tomarías (you would take)....

    a. el arte   b. la química   c. la educación física   d. el latín

2. Si te gusta cantar, tomarías (you would take)....

    a. la economía doméstica   b. el calculo   c. el coro   d. la informática

3. Si te gusta hacer ejercicios, tomarías (you would take)....

    a. la educación física   b. la física   c. el inglés   d. el salón de estudios

4. Si te gustan las matemáticas, tomarías (you would take)....

    a. el almuerzo   b. la biología   c. el álgebra   d. el alemán

5. Si te gusta leer, tomarías (you would take)....

    a. el francés   b. la geometría   c. las ciencias sociales   d. la lectura

Exercise 2.1e:

Directions: Read the paragraph. Then, answer the questions.

Éste es el horario de Arturo. A las 9:30, tiene la trigonometría. Después, tiene la física y la informática. El almuerzo es a las 12:00. A las 1:15, tiene el laboratorio de ciencias. Al fin del día, estudia el cálculo.

How many classes does Arturo take?   _____

When does Arturo have lunch?   _____

What career path do you think Arturo will take?   _____

Ejercicios

Exercise 2.1f:

Directions: Translate into Spanish. You will need to be creative and use prior knowledge.

1. Do you study German?   _____

2. What is your schedule?   _____

3. Do you have many classes?   _____

4. How many science classes do you have?   _____

5. This is my schedule.   _____

SECTION 2.2 - WHAT JUST HAPPENED?

■ DAY 1

OBJECTIVES

You will learn to:
- To describe classes

Describing Classes

Now that you know how to say what classes you have, you probably want to know how to talk a little bit about them. This lesson is designed to provide you with the necessary vocabulary to give a general description of your classes.

Adjectives

Divertido	Amusing/fun
Interesante	Interesting
Aburrido	Boring
Difícil	Difficult
Fácil	Easy
Complicado	Complicated
Bueno	Good
Malo	Bad
Grande	Big
Pequeño	Small

Adjusting Placement and Agreement

Let's review how to use adjectives. As you previously learned, words that describe nouns are referred to as adjectives. You can also review adjective agreement by reading the initial lessons of Unit IV in Part 1 of Spanish 1.

1. Adjectives are placed after nouns.

El francés es una clase aburrida.   French is a boring class.
noun   adjective

2. Adjectives must agree, in number and gender, with the noun they describe.

La clase es pequeña.   The class is small.

(Because the word "clase" is singular and feminine the adjective is in the singular and feminine form. Therefore, "pequeña" ends in the letter -a.)

Las clases son pequeñas.   The classes are small.

(Because the word "clases" is plural and feminine, the adjective is in the plural and feminine form. Therfore, "pequeñas" ends in the letters -as.)

El francés es aburrido.   French is boring.

(Because the word "francés" is singular and masculine, the adjective is in the singular and masculine form. Therefore, "aburrido" ends in the letter -o.)

El francés y el latín son aburridos.   French and Latin are boring.

(Because the words, "francés" and "latín," are plural and masculine, the adjective is in the masculine plural form. Therefore, "aburridos" ends in the letters -os.)

Examples:

¿Cómo es la clase?	What is the class like?
La informática es interesante, buena y fácil.	Computing is interesting, good and easy.
También, el latín es interesante, bueno, y fácil.	Latin is also interesting, good, and easy.
¿Cómo son las clases?	What are the classes like?
Las clases son divertidas y fáciles.	The classes are fun and easy.

■ DAY 2

OBJECTIVES

You will learn to:
   – To say that something just happened

What just happened?

When you want to say something just happened, you would use the verb "acabar" followed by the preposition "de" and an infinitive in Spanish. You would conjugate the verb in the present tense, although the action occurred in the past.

Acabar de ___ - To Just _____

Yo acabo de – I just	Nosotros Nosotras acabamos de - We just
Tú acabas de - You just	Vosotros Vosotras acabáis de - All of you just
Él acaba de - He just Ella She just Usted (Ud.) You (formal) just	Ellos acaban de - They just Ellas Ustedes (Uds.) All of you just

Examples:

Acabo de tener clase.   I just had class.

Acabamos de estudiar el español.   I just studied Spanish.

Acaban de comer.   They just ate.

 Nota Cultural

Types of Schools in Spain

In Spain, students follow this plan of study for their schooling.

Type of School	Definition	Age of Student
El Preescolar	**Preschool**	**3-5**
La Guardería	Nursery School	3-4
El Jardín de la Infancia	Kindergarten	5
La Educación Básica	**Basic Education**	**6-16**
La Escuela Primaria	Primary School	6-11
La Enseñanza Secundaria	Secondary School	12- 16
El Bachillerato	**Preparation for College**	**16-18**
Las Universidades	**University, College, or Vocational Training**	**18- 23+**
Los colegios universitarios	Vocational or Non-academic Study	18- 21+
Las escuelas universitarias	Academic Study	18- 21+
Las facultades	Academic Study	18- 23+

Ejercicios

Exercise 2.2a:

Directions: Unscramble the letters to reveal the adjective. Then, write the meaning of that adjective in the space provided.

	Word	Meaning
1. e t i n e t e t n a s r	_____	_____
2. á i l f c	_____	_____
3. d o i t r e v i d	_____	_____
4. rr b d o i u a	_____	_____
5. c i l f i d í	_____	_____

Exercise 2.2b:

Directions: Circle whether the statements are Lógica (Logical) or Ilógica (Illogical).

1. No le gusta la clase de arte nada porque es divertida.
   Lógica   Ilógica

2. Hay 5 estudiantes en la clase de alemán; es una clase pequeña.
   Lógica   Ilógica

3. La clase es muy difícil porque tenemos mucha tarea y exámenes.
   Lógica   Ilógica

4. No hacemos nada en la clase de inglés; es aburrida.
   Lógica   Ilógica

5. La clase es grande cuando tenemos 32 personas.
   Lógica   Ilógica

Ejercicios

Exercise 2.2c:

Directions: Answer the questions ia a full sentence in Spanish based on your own schedule.

Information	Question	Response

1. ¿Cómo es la geometría? _____

_____

_____

2. ¿Cómo son el coro y el arte? _____

_____

3. ¿A qué hora es la química?_____

_____

_____

4. ¿Es el francés interesante?_____

_____

_____

Exercise 2.2d:

Directions: Translate the following.

1. I just had class.   _____

2. We just studied for the exam.   _____

3. My friends just went to the mall.   _____

4. My mom just walked the dog.   _____

5. All of you just did the homework.   _____

Ejercicios

Exercise 2.2e:

Directions: Put the sentences in chronological order.

1. ____, ____, ____, _____

    a. Acabo de ir al cine.
    b. Voy a ir al cine.
    c. Voy al cine.
    d. Estoy en al cine.

2. ____, ____, ____, _____, _____

    a. Juan acaba de salir al parque.
    b. Juan vuelve a casa.
    c. Juan quiere ir al parque.
    d. Juan sale de su casa.
    e. Juan va al parque.

Exercise 2.2f:

Directions: Match the school with the student.

1. ____ Marcos, 10   a. Va a una guardería.

2. ____ Carolina, 15   b. Va para el bachillerato.

3. ____ Ana Maria, 4   c. Va a la escuela primaria.

4. ____ David, 19   d. Va a una enseñanza secundaria.

5. ____ Flor, 17   e. Va a la Universidad.

SECTION 2.3 - CLASS SEQUENCE

■ DAY 1

OBJECTIVES

You will learn:

- To list ordinal numbers

- To state order of classes

- To abbreviate ordinal numbers

Class Sequence

When you receive your schedule of classes, they are arranged in a series, or order. Your classes can be numbered according to how they are scheduled. You may sequence them from your first class to your last class. In order to be able to sequence classes, or any list, you must learn some ordinal numbers.

Because ordinal numbers are also adjectives that modify nouns, they must agree in number and gender. The list of ordinal numbers below will be in the masculine singular.

To make the ordinal numbers agree with:

- Nouns that are feminine and singular, add "-a."

Ordinal Numbers

Primer	First
Segundo	Second
Tercer	Third
Cuarto	Fourth
Quinto	Fifth
Sexto	Sixth
Séptimo	Seventh
Octavo	Eighth
Noveno	Ninth
Décimo	Tenth
En la _____ hora	In _____ period

Examples:

En mi primera clase, yo tengo mucha tarea.	In my first class, I have a lot of homework.
El primer día es muy interesante.	The first day is very interesting.
En la octava hora, tengo la música.	In eighth period, I have music.
El octavo estudiante es Rodolfo.	The eighth student is Rodolfo.

Abbreviating Ordinal Numbers

In Spanish, you do not abbreviate the ordinal numbers the same way you would in English. You would use "-o" or "-a" in superscript after the number.

El tercer piso	-	1º piso	The third floor
La tercera hora	-	1ª hora	The third period

■ DAY 2

OBJECTIVES

You will learn to:
- To list transition words
- To sequence classes
- To ask class sequence

Another Way to Sequence Classes

When you want to sequence your classes, you don't always have to put them in numerical order. You can use transition words to link your sentences together as well. Transition words are words that connect one idea to another in sentences, paragraphs, or longer bodies of writing. This list of some common transition words in Spanish will provide words that will help you combine your thoughts.

Transition Words

Antes (de)	Before ("de" is used when "antes" occurs in a phrase)
Después (de)	After ("de" is used when "después" occurs in a phrase)
Entonces	Thus/then
Luego	Then/ afterwards/ next
No obstante	However
Por ejemplo	For example
Por fin	Finally
Próximo	Next
También	Also

Examples:

Antes de salir, necesito hacer la tarea.	Before leaving, I need to do my homework.
Después, tengo las ciencias.	After, I have science.
Después de la informática, tengo las ciencias.	After computing, I have science.
Tengo un examen mañana; no obstante, voy a la fiesta.	I have an exam tomorrow; however, I am going to the party.
Tengo la clase de álgebra por fin.	I have algebra class last.

 Nota Cultural

School Uniforms

In the U.S., until recently, school uniforms have only been typical in private schools. However, in the rest of the world many students wear school uniforms.

For example, in Mexico, Central America, and many Spanish speaking countries of South America, it is typical to see students wearing uniforms. This is also true in Spain.

Ejercicios

Exercise 2.3a:

Directions: Someone dropped their papers. Reorder them based on the ordinal numbers.

a. Qunito

b. Segundo

c. Décimo

d. Octavo

e. Cuarto

f. Primer

g. Séptimo

h. Noveno

i. Tercer

j. Sexto

Reorder: _____

Ejercicios

Exercise 2.3b:

Directions: Write a paragraph that tells what periods Vivian has each class. Spell the ordinal numbers. Use the example as a model for your sentences.

Example: En la primera hora, Vivian tiene el inglés.

Hora	Clase
1ª	Inglés
2ª	Español
3ª	Biología
4ª	Coro
5ª	Almuerzo
6ª	Educación Física
7ª	Matemáticas
8ª	Salón de Estudios
9ª	Informática
10ª	Arte

_____

_____

_____

_____

_____

_____

_____

_____

_____

_____

Ejercicios

Exercise 2.3c:

Directions: Correct the errors.

1. Es el primero día de clases.   _____

2. En la cuarto hora, tiene el coro.   _____

3. Es la 8th clase.   _____

4. Tiene el español en la 2nd hora.   _____

Exercise 2.3d:

Directions: Number the sentences so that they are in correct order.

_____ Luego, tengo el almuerzo.

_____ Por fin, tengo el salón de estudios.

_____ Primero, tengo la clase de francés.

_____ Después del almuerzo, tengo el inglés.

_____ Próximo, tengo las matemáticas.

Exercise 2.3e:

Directions: Place each of the vocabulary words from the Word Bank correctly in the blanks of the sentences. There may be more than one possible correct answer.

Word Bank

Antes   Después   No obstante   Por ejemplo   También

1. Tengo mucha tarea; _____, no me molesta porque
    voy a pasar tiempo con mis amigos esta tarde.

2. Ella tiene dos hermanos; _____, yo tengo dos hermanos.

3. Me gusta mucho ayudar a mi madre en casa. _____,
    yo saco la basura y lavo la ropa.

4. Tengo que estudiar _____ de tomar el examen mañana.

5. Tengo el arte a las 11:00. _____, tengo el alemán a las 12:00.

Ejercicios

Exercise 2.3f:

Directions: Translate the following sentences.

1. After reading, I have science.
2. Then, I have Spanish.
3. I like art; however, I don't have art class.
4. He is really intelligent; for example, he studies physics.
5. Before going, I want to eat.

_____

_____

_____

_____

_____

SECTION 2.4 - "FAVORITE" PEOPLE AT SCHOOL

■ DAY 1

You will learn:

- To list the people at school with their proper titles
- To ask and answer questions about people

People at School

Schools are filled with people who receive and offer educational and community services. In this section, you will learn the vocabulary for the names of these professionals. In addition, you will also learn how to refer to these people in conversation.

People at School

Alumno/a	Student
Estudiante	
Asesor/a académico/a	Counselor
Consejero/a académico/a	
Asistente de maestro	Teacher's assistant
Bibliotecario/a	Librarian
Conductor/a de autobús	Bus driver
Conserje	Janitor
Director/a	Principal
Enfermero/a	Nurse
Entrenador/a	Coach
Maestro/a	Teacher
Profesor/a	
Secretario/a	Secretary
Subdirector/a	Vice-principal
Trabajador/a de la cafetería	Cafeteria worker
Trabajador/a social	Social worker

Addressing School Professionals

Although people fall into one of these service categories, it is not typical to address people by that category. For example, you would not call to someone, "librarian." Instead, you would call the person by his/her title of: Mr., Miss, Mrs. or Doctor.

Here's how you would say the titles for these people. The abbreviations for each title are in parenthesis.

Señor (Sr.)	Mr.
Señorita (Srta.)	Miss
Señora (Sra.)	Mrs.
Doctor (Dr.)	Doctor (male)
Doctora (Dra.)	Doctor (female)

Examples:

Hola, Srta. Aguilera.   Hello, Miss Aguilera.

Perdón, Sr., necesito ayuda.   Excuse me, Mr., I need help.

If you were not speaking directly to the person, but instead speaking of the person, you would need to place an "el" or "la" in front of the title.

El Sr. Sánchez es mi profesor de español.   Mr. Sanchez is my Spanish teacher.

La Dra. Peris es mi profesora.   Dr. Peris is my teacher.

■ DAY 2

OBJECTIVES

You will learn to:
  - To express favorites

Favorites

One topic that is often of interest to people is "favorite things." It is interesting to talk about favorite teachers, classes, and activities. In this lesson, you will learn to express favorites.

There are two adjectives that are used to express that something is a favorite.

Favorito

Preferido   Favorite

Review

Nouns are either masculine or feminine. Feminine nouns typically end in "-a," "-ción," or "-tad." Masculine nouns end in "-o" or any other letter, although there are exceptions.

Adjectives that modify masculine nouns typically end in "-o."
Adjectives that modify feminine nouns typically end in "-a."

To make nouns and their adjectives plural, add the letter "-s." Let's look at some examples.

Examples:

Masculine-
    Singular
                El libro es mi favorito.   The book is my favorite.
    Plural
                Los libros son mis favoritos.   The books are my favorites.

Feminine-
    Singular
                La revista es mi favorita.   The magazine is my favorite.
    Plural
                Las revistas son mis favoritas.   The magazines are my favorites.

As you know, adjectives directly follow the noun they modify, or describe. In the next set of examples, you can see adjective placement with nouns that are masculine/feminine and singular/plural.

Masculine-
    Singular
                Es mi libro favorito.   It is my favorite book.
    Plural
                Son mis libros favoritos.   They are my favorite books.

Feminine-
    Singular
                Es mi revista favorita.   It is my favorite magazine.
    Plural
                Son mis revistas favoritas.   They are my favorite magazines.

 Nota Cultural

Grading Scale

The grading scale varies in many countries. In Mexico, the grading scale is from 1-10 with 1 being the lowest score and 10 being the highest.

A passing score is a 6. Students who do not achieve a minimum score of 6 on the national exam are retained for the next school year. The national exam is based on the grade level curricula which are taught to all students in Mexico.

Ejercicios

Exercise 2.4a:

Directions: Match the person to the activity.

1. ___ el conserje
2. ___ el alumno
3. ___ la trabajadora de la cafetería

4. ___ la bibliotecaria
5. ___ la asistente de maestro

6. ___ la secretaria
7. ___ el maestro

a. enseña a los estudiantes.
b. saca la basura.
c. lee mucho y presta los libros a los estudiantes.
d. estudia mucho.
e. usa la computadora y ayuda a los directores.
f. ayuda al maestro.
g. prepara la comida.

Exercise 2.4b:

Directions: Based on the conversation, answer the questions.

Ernesto: Hola. ¿Tienes clases aquí? ¿Cómo es tu horario?
Pilar: Sí, estoy matriculado en clases. Mi horario es complicado.
Ernesto: ¿Qué clases tienes?
Pilar: En la primera hora, tengo las ciencias sociales.
Ernesto: ¿Quién es el profesor?
Pilar: La Sra. Ramos Ortega es la profesora.
Ernesto: Ella es una profesora estricta y la clase es muy difícil.
Pilar: ¡Qué horrible!
Ernesto: ¿Cuándo tienes el almuerzo?
Pilar: En la sexta hora. Después de mi clase de educación física.
Ernesto: ¿Tienes la clase de educación física en la quinta hora? Yo también.
Pilar: ¿Con el Sr. Gonzáles?
Ernesto: Claro, con el Sr. Gonzáles.
Pilar: Excelente.
Ernesto: ¿Qué hora es? Mi clase de español es a las 2:00.
Pilar: ¡Son las 2:05 ahora!
Ernesto: ¡Ay, no! Llego tarde. Tengo que irme.
Pilar: Adiós. Hasta pronto.
Ernesto: Chao.

1. ¿Van Pilar y Ernesto a la misma (same) escuela?   _____

2. ¿Quiénes son los profesores de Pilar?   _____

3. ¿Qué clases tienen ellos en la quinta hora?   _____

4. ¿Cómo es la Sra. Ramos Ortega?   _____

5. ¿Adónde va Ernesto?   _____

Ejercicios

Exercise 2.4c:

Directions: Based on the school directory, write a sentence in Spanish telling each person's position. Follow the example.

Directory of Employees
(Listed in Alphabetical Order)

Last Name	Title	Extension
Ackers, Mr.	Teacher, Reading	x8516
Adams, Mrs.	Vice-principal	x8422
Allegro, Mr.	Coach, Tennis	x8968
Amante, Miss	Social Worker	x8424
Apache, Dr.	Counselor, A-L	x8423
Arnez, Mrs.	Driver, Bus	x8712 (bus garage)

Example: El Sr. Ackers es el profesor de lectura.

1. _____

2. _____

3. _____

4. _____

5. _____

Exercise 2.4d:

Directions: Translate the sentences.

1. Math class is my favorite.   _____

2. Art is my favorite class.   _____

3. Mr. López is my favorite teacher.   _____

4. They are my favorite.   _____

5. It is not my favorite.   _____

Ejercicios

Exercise 2.4e:

Directions: *Compare the grading scale in Mexico to one in the U.S.*

Mexico

10
9
8
7
6
Below 6 = Failure
5
4
3
2
1

U.S.

100 – 90	= A
89-80	= B
79-70	= C
69-60	= D
59-0	= F/E

Comparison: _____

_____

Section 2.5 - School Items and Objects

■ Day 1

OBJECTIVES

You will learn:
- To list class objects/school items
- To locate class objects/school items

School Items

There are many items that you usually use for school. Think of what you need daily to complete your assignments or do work. By the end of this section, you will be able to express the school items you regularly use.

School Items

El bolígrafo	The pen
La pluma	
La calculadora	The calculator
La carpeta	The folder/binder
La computadora	The computer
El cuaderno	The notebook
El cuaderno de ejercicios	The workbook
El diccionario	The dictionary
La goma de borrar	The eraser
La hoja de papel	The piece of paper
La impresora	The printer (for a computer)
El lápiz	The pencil
El libro	The book
La mochila	The book bag
El papel	The paper
La regla	The ruler
El sacapuntas	The pencil sharpener

How Many?

In Unit 3, you already learned how to say, "How many." In addition, you learned the words for "many," "some," and "few." You are expected to review and be able to express how many of each school item you have.

In addition to being able to give the general amount, in this section you will learn to give the specific amount of an item. For example, you will learn how to say, "Three pencils" or "21 books."

Expressing Specific Quantity

To express specific quantity, you would first need to remove the definite or indefinite article in front of the noun. Then, you would add the number. If the number is plural, of course your noun must also be plural.

El libro   (original)

libro   (remove article)

15 libros   (add quantity)

It's easy, right? However, you must learn how to place a number with "1" in front of nouns.

The number 1 is expressed in front of nouns as "un" or "una." These vocabulary words can also mean "a/an" as you may remember from a previous section.

Un libro   1 book, a book

Una carpeta   1 folder, a folder

When numbers increase, but are still a denomination with 1, you must express the number 1, in front of a noun, the same way.

Veintiún libros   21 books

Veintiuna carpetas   21 folders

Cuarenta y un papeles   41 papers

Cincuenta y una reglas   51 rulers

■ DAY 2

OBJECTIVES

You will learn to:
- To list class objects/school items
- To locate class objects/ school items

Class Objects

Many classrooms are arranged with similar furniture and decorations. When you enter into most classrooms, it is typical to see student and teacher desks, a flag, and other items conducive to a working school environment. You will be able to name and locate these items by the end of this section.

Class Objects

El armario	The closet
La bandera	The flag
El cartel	The poster
El escritorio	The desk (teacher)
El estante	The book shelf
Las luces de techo	The ceiling light
La pared	The wall
El perchero	The coat rack
La pizarra	The chalkboard
La puerta	The door
El pupitre	The student desk
La silla	The chair
El suelo	The floor
El tablón de anuncios	The bulletin board
El techo	The ceiling
La ventana	The window
El aula	The classroom
El salón de clases	The classroom

 Nota Cultural

Did you ever wonder what students from Spanish-Speaking countries looked like? Or, did you ever want to see their classrooms and where they study?

These pictures will give you a snap shot of students and classrooms in Spanish-Speaking countries.

Ejercicios

Exercise 2.5a:

Directions: Write the vocabulary word for the item/s you would use to complete each task.

1. You need to add problems in Math class. _____
2. You made a mistake and need to erase. _____
3. You need to look up vocabulary words. _____
4. You need to write something. _____
5. You need to read something. _____
6. You need to draw a straight line. _____
7. You need to sharpen your pencil. _____

Exercise 2.5b:

Directions: Write a sentence telling how many of each item there is/are. Follow the example.

Example: Hay 2 plumas.

1.    _____

2.    _____

3.    _____

4. _____

5. _____

Ejercicios

Exercise 2.5c:

Directions: *Match the English to the Spanish. Not all letters will be used.*

1. ____61 sheets of paper   a. diez y una plumas
2. ____81 papers   b. once plumas
3. ____71 books   c. sesenta y una hojas de papel
4. ____21 book bags   d. cincuenta y un bolígrafos
5. ____31 pens   e. treinta y una plumas
6. ____51 pens   f. veintiuna mochilas
7. ____11 pens   g. setenta y uno libros
                                h. ochenta y un papeles
                                i. setenta y un libros

Exercise 2.5d:

Directions: *Draw a picture to illustrate the classroom described in the paragraph.*

En la clase de ciencias sociales, hay veinte pupitres con sillas. El escritorio para la Sra. Álvarez está enfrente de los pupitres. A la izquierda, hay un estante y un tablón de anuncios. A la derecha, hay un perchero y una bandera de los Estados Unidos. Detrás de los pupitres, hay una pizarra. En el techo, hay dos luces de techo. No hay ventanas. Hay una puerta a la derecha de la pizarra.

Ejercicios

Exercise 2.5e:

Directions: Fill in the vocabulary word. Then, solve the "secret phrase."

1. The coat rack   PHCEORELE   □□□□□□□□□
                                                    7

2. The flag   BANRALAED   □□□□□□□□□
                                                   11

3. The floor   ESLELUO   □□□□□□□
                                          1 10

4. The book shelf   LETSEENAT   □□□□□□□□
                                             6   4

5. The bulletin board   NAINATLOUBOSDELNEC □□□□□□□□□□□□□□□□□
                                                3   8   9

6. The wall   RAELAPD   □□□□□□□
                                              2

7. The chalkboard   RIAPAZRAL   □□□□□□□□□
                                              5

□□□□□□□□□ F □
1 2 3 4 5 6 7 8 9   10 11

Exercise 2.5f:

Directions: Translate the sentence into Spanish.

1. The room has a ceiling, floor, and four walls. _____

2. There is a bookshelf and a coat rack.   _____

3. I am writing on the chalkboard.   _____

4. I need to put the clothes in the closet.   _____

5. We have a flag of Mexico.   _____

NOTES

Section 2.1

_____ Date

Section 2.2

_____ Date

Section 2.3

_____ Date

Section 2.4 _____ Date

Section 2.5 _____ Date

Additional Notes _____ Date

SECTION 2.6 - MISSING ITEMS

■ DAY 1

You will learn:

- To state what's missing/lacking
- To express another way to say need

Missing School Items

Have you ever misplaced something for school? Or, have you ever needed something and just don't have it? Or, have you ever missed a homework assignment or forgot something important for school? If any of these situations sounds familiar, you are going to find this section pertinent. In this section, you will learn how to say that something is missing or lacking.

Missing School Items

To express that something is missing or lacking, you would use the verb "faltar." "Faltar" is conjugated just like "gustar;" so, if you remember how to use the different forms of "gustar" in a sentence, you will learn the verb "faltar" quickly. If not, "no te preocupes" (don't worry). This section will teach you everything you need to know.

There are four interpretations for the translation of "faltar." It is typical to choose the best translation for the situation. You will see how the conjugate verb is used in the sentence below, as well as the four possible meanings for the sentence.

Me falta un lápiz.	I am missing a pencil.
	I lack a pencil.
	I need a pencil.
	I don't have a pencil.

In this example, three of the four possible translations make sense and can be applied to a situation where someone would be without a pencil.

Falta versus Faltan

Two forms of "faltar" are typically used to state need: "falta" or "faltan." You would use "falta" when someone is missing only one thing. "Faltan" is used when two or more things are missing.

Me falta mi libro.	I am missing my book.
	I lack my book.
	I need my book.
	I don't have my book.

Me faltan mis libros.	I am missing my books.
	I lack my books.
	I need my books.
	I don't have my books.

Me faltan mi libro y mi lápiz.	I am missing my book and my pencil.
	I lack my books and my pencil.
	I need my books and my pencil.
	I don't have my book or my pencil.

■ Day 2

OBJECTIVES

You will learn to:

- To state what others are missing/ lacking
- To ask what others are missing/ lacking

Other People's Missing Items

You don't always have to be the person missing items. You can express that others also misplace, lack, need, or don't have items. The chart below provides additional indirect object pronouns that accompany the verb.

Faltar- To miss; to lack

Form of Falta/n		Form of Falta/n	
Me falta/n	I miss or lack	Nos falta/n	We miss or lack
Te falta/n	You miss or lack	Os falta/n	All of you miss or lack
Le falta/n	He/she misses or lacks You (formal) miss or lack	Les falta/n	They miss or lack All of you miss or lack

Examples:

Le faltan muchas cosas.	He is missing many things.
Nos falta la tarea.	We're missing the homework.
Les faltan sus horarios de clases.	They are missing their class schedules.

Using Someone's Name

You can also clarify, with a name, the person or people who are missing something. Again, the pattern is the same as the "gustar" pattern. You would place an "a" before the person's name.

A Simón le falta el libro.	Simon is missing the book.
A Pilar y a Xavier les faltan las llaves.	Pilar and Xavier are missing the keys.

Asking What's Missing

Follow the pattern below to ask what's missing.

¿Qué te falta?	What are you missing?
¿Qué le falta a Juan?	What is Juan missing?
¿Qué nos faltan?	What are we missing (more than one thing)?

 Nota Cultural

Los Sinónimos

A synonym is a word having the same, or almost the same, meaning as another word in the same language. Just as in the English language, Spanish is filled with synonyms. It is important to recognize some synonyms for words that you already know.

Word	Synonym	Meaning
El afiche	El cartel	The poster
El aparador	El armario	The closet
El asiento	La silla	The chair
El objeto	La cosa	The thing/ the object
El póster	El cartel	The poster
El ropero	El armario	The closet

Ejercicios

Exercise 2.6a:

Directions: Fill in "falta" or "faltan" to complete the sentence.

1. Me _____ los cuadernos.
2. Me _____ el libro de español.
3. Me _____ mucho papel.
4. Me _____ mis papeles.
5. Me _____ una calculadora para la clase de matemáticas.

Exercise 2.6b:

Directions: Write a sentence in Spanish stating the item you are missing.

1. A pencil and an eraser _____

2. The book bag _____

3. The homework _____

4. The rulers _____

5. A folder _____

Exercise 2.6c:

Directions: Read the email. Then, answer the questions.

Margarita,

Voy al centro comercial hoy porque me faltan muchas cosas para el primer día de clases. No puedo encontrar unas cosas escolares que acabo de tener. Me falta mi mochila. Y, me faltan un diccionario y mi calculadora.

¿Necesitas comprar algo? ¿Quieres ir conmigo?

- Rodolfo

1. ¿Por qué va Rodolfo al centro comercial?

   _____

2. ¿Qué le faltan?

   _____

3. ¿Invita Rodolfo a Margarita?

   _____

Ejercicios

Exercise 2.6e:

Directions: Match the Spanish to the English.

1. _____ Le falta.   A. You're missing it.
2. _____ Nos falta.   B. They're missing it.
3. _____ Os falta.   C. He/she is missing it.
4. _____ Te falta.   D. All of you are missing it.
5. _____ Les falta.   E. We're missing it.

Exercise 2.6e:

Directions: Based on the pictures, answer the questions.

1. ¿Qué te falta?   _____

2. ¿Qué le faltan a Julio?   _____

3. ¿Qué nos faltan?   _____

4. ¿Qué les falta?   _____

5. ¿Qué os faltan?   _____

Ejercicios

Exercise 2.6f:

Directions: Fill in the analogy with correct word in Spanish.

1. "El ropero" is to "el armario" as _____ is to "la silla."

2. "El poster" is to "el cartel" as _____ is to "el cartel."

3. "Notebook" is to "el cuaderno" as _____ is to "el agenda."

4. "La cosa" is to _____ as "el aparador" is to "el armario."

5. "El ordenador" is to _____ as "la pluma" is to "el bolígrafo."

SECTION 2.7 - ROOMS IN A SCHOOL

■ DAY 1

You will learn to:

- To list rooms in a school
- To state the use of the rooms
- To give location and direction of the rooms

Rooms in a School

A school is filled with other rooms than classes. If you wanted to take classes at an educational institution that includes an on-site learning facility, you may find that the site includes an office, fitness and performing arts area, as well as other rooms or departments. In this section, you will learn the names for each of these areas.

Rooms in a School

El auditorio	The auditorium
El aula*	The classroom
La biblioteca	The library
La cafetería	The cafeteria
El casillero (escolar)	The (school) locker
El comedor	The lunch room
La enfermería	The nurse's office (station)
La entrada	The entrance (hallway)
El gimnasio	The gymnasium
El laboratorio (de investigación)	The laboratory
La oficina	The office
El salón (de clases)	The classroom
El vestíbulo	The hallway
El vestuario	The locker room

*Aula uses the masculine article el, but it is actually a feminine noun. El is used instead of la to avoid the two "a" sounds running together in la aula. Since it is a feminine noun, any adjectives that modify the noun will also have to be feminine. For example: El aula es pequeña= The classroom is small.

Rooms Uses

One way to state how rooms are used is to use the phrases, "se usa" or "se usan." In later lessons, you will learn the grammatical purpose for the "se" in front of the verb "usar." The meaning of "se usa" or "se usan" translates to "is used." The difference between the two phrases is that "se usa" is used for a singular place or thing and "se usan" is used for more than one place or thing.

Examples:

Se usa el comedor para comer.	The lunch room is used to eat.
Se usan las aulas para tener clase.	The classrooms are used to have class.
Se usa un lápiz para escribir.	A pencil is used to write.

■ DAY 2

OBJECTIVES

You will learn to:
- To describe places or things
- To define the grammatical term "participle"
- To use estar + participles (regular only)

Describing Places or Things with Past Participles

As you already know, you can use adjectives to describe or modify nouns. However, other parts of speech can be used as adjectives to describe nouns. One part of speech, that will be the topic of this section, is the past participle. Spanish and English both have participles; and, in both languages, participles are known to follow patterns.
In English, the past participle is a form of a non-conjugated verb. That form has generally has and -en or -ed at the end of it. Let's look at some examples in English. Can you think of others?

Past Participles in English

Spoken	Used	Scheduled	Eaten
Talked	Worked	Listened	Been
Closed	Driven	Washed	Seen
Opened	Taken	Watched	Walked

In Spanish, the past participle is also a form of a non-conjugated verb. To form the past participle in Spanish, follow these steps:

Formation of the Past Participles

1. Start with the infinitive.
2. Then, drop the -ar, -er, or -ir form of the verb.
3. Add -ado for -ar verbs and -ido for -er and -ir verbs.

Of course, just as in English, exceptions exist. You will learn those in the future. For now, let's look at some examples with verb you already know.

Past Participles in Spanish

-AR VERBS	-ER and -IR VERBS
(-ar to -ado)	*(-er or -ir to -ido)*
Encontrar → encontrado	aprender → aprendido
To find → found	to learn → learned
Hablar → hablado	beber → bebido
To speak → spoken	to drink → drunk
Lavar → lavado	compartir → compartido
To wash → washed	to share → shared
Usar → usado	recibir → recibido
To use → used	to receive → received
Estudiar → estudiado	leer → leído*
To study → studied	to read → read

(*accented to retain syllabication and pronunciation)

Important Clarification

- DO NOT GET CONFUSED: PAST PARTIPLES ARE NOT CONJUGATED VERBS!!!

    You CANNOT say anything like:

    Yo recibido una carta.

    It DOES NOT MEAN:

    I received a letter.

- Past Participles are typically used WITH a conjugated verb for the following reasons:

    - to describe

    - to form part of a verb tense.

- YOU TYPICALLY DO NOT USE PAST PARTICIPLES ALONE.

Estar + Past Participle

Estar + past participle is used to describe how things are at the moment, in a temporary state. The description of the item is not necessarily permanent. For example, in the sentence, "the door is closed," the past participle "closed" is used with a conjugated form of "estar." The door is not always going to be closed, but the temporary description of the door at this moment is that it is closed. In Spanish, the sentence would be expressed as, "la puerta está cerrada."

Are you wondering, "why does 'cerrada' end in –ada, and not –ado?" Well, that's an excellent question. When past participles are used as adjectives, they must agree in number and gender with the noun they modify. So, the past participle for –ar verbs can be: –ado, -ada, -ados, and -adas, depending on the noun it modifies. Also, the past participle for –er and –ir verbs can be: -ido, -ida, -idos, and –idas. Let's look at some examples.

Examples:

El libro está encontrado.	The book is found.
Los libros están encontrados.	The books are found.
La mochila está encontrada.	The book bag is found.
Las mochilas están encontradas.	The book bags are found.

Some New Verbs

Here is a list of some verbs that are commonly used as past participles. You will learn others in the next sections.

Cerrar → cerrado
> To close → closed

Situar → situado
> To situate/locate → situated/located

Ubicar → ubicado
> To situate/locate → situated/located

Cambiar → cambiado
> To change → changed

Perder → Perdido
> To lose → lost

Nota Cultural

Past Participles in Expressions

Past participles also can occur in expressions. Past participles also can occur in idiomatic expressions. Idiomatic expressions are groups of words that have a certain meaning when grouped together, but this meaning is different from the dictionary meaning of each of the individual words. For example, "across the board" (meaning that something applies to everyone) is an idiom. Other English idioms are "a bit much" and "all set" (meaning 'ready').

The following expressions use some of the past participles from this lesson. Notice how in each of these expressions the past participle is used as an adjective.

Expressions

Estar muy bien situado- to have a good position.

Example: Estoy bien situado en mi trabajo.   I have a good position at work.

Ser tonto perdido - to be completely stupid

Example: Esta chica es tonta perdida.   That girl is completely stupid.

Estar a puerta cerrada- to be behind closed doors

Example: El negocio está a puerta cerrada. The business deal is behind closed.

Tener intereses encontrados - to have conflicting interests

Example: Porque tiene intereses encontrados no sabe que hacer. Because he has conflicting interests, he doesn't know what to do.

Ejercicios

Exercise 2.7a:

Directions: Label the rooms in Spanish as well.

Gym					
Locker Room					
Lunch Room	Hallway				Lockers
Library	Nurse's Office	Lab	Classrooms		Auditorium

Exercise 2.7b:

Directions: Fill in the blanks with the "se usa" or "se usan."

1. _____ el dinero para comprar cosas.
2. _____ los laboratorios para hacer experimentos.
3. _____ el gimnasio para la clase de educación física.
4. _____ las aulas para tener clase.
5. _____ el comedor para almorzar.

Ejercicios

Exercise 2.7c:

Directions: Based on the drawing, answer the questions. Please review prior lessons for directional vocabulary. Follow the example.

Example: ¿Dónde está la oficina?
                        La oficina está cerca del vestíbulo.

El aula 101	Los casilleros	El aula 201
El laboratorio	El vestíbulo	El gimnasio
El aula 103	La oficina	El vestuario

1. ¿Dónde está el gimnasio?
2. ¿Dónde está el aula 101?
3. ¿Dónde están los casilleros?
4. ¿Dónde está el vestuario?
5. ¿Dónde está el laboratorio?

Exercise 2.7d:

Directions: Form the past participle. Then, write the meaning of the past participle.

	Past Participle	Meaning
1. Cambiar →	_____	_____
2. Aburrir →	_____	_____
3. Situar →	_____	_____
4. Perder →	_____	_____
5. Organizar →	_____	_____
6. Compartir →	_____	_____
7. Beber →	_____	_____
8. Divorciar →	_____	_____
9. Frustrar →	_____	_____
10. Divertir →	_____	_____

Ejercicios

Exercise 2.7e:

Directions: Write out the sentence in Spanish. Remember: use a form of "estar" for your verb.

1. The door is closed.

   _____

2. The dog is lost.

   _____

3. The classrooms are located near my locker.

   _____

4. The clothes are washed and cleaned.

   _____

5. The nurse's office is located next to the auditorium.

   _____

Exercise 2.7f:

Directions: Write whether the statement is Correct or Incorrect on the line. If the statement is incorrect, correct it.

1. _____ Words that ends in –ado, -edo, or –ido are past participles in the Spanish language.
2. _____ To form the past participle of an -ar verb, simply add -ado.
3. _____ Words that end in -ed or -en are past participles in English.
4. _____ A past participle can be used in place of conjugated verbs.
5. _____ A past participle can be used as an adjective.
6. _____ A past participle can help to form another verb tense.
7. _____ When used as adjectives, past participles must agree with the noun they modify.

SECTION 2.8 – EXPRESSING THE PAST (USING PAST PARTICIPLES)

■ DAY 1

You will learn:
- To express past actions
- To recognize and form the present perfect tense

Expressing Past Action Using Past Participles

One way to express actions that have occurred in the past is to use the present perfect tense. The present perfect tense is called a compound tense because it is formed by two verbs- a main verb and an auxiliary verb, or "helper" verb.

The helper verb is always "haber," followed by a past participle (the main verb). If you remember from the last lesson, a past participle is a non-conjugated form of a verb that ends in -ado or -ido.

A general translation of the present perfect tense would be "has/have" + verb (has done, has read, etc.). The reasons below will give you an idea of when the present perfect tense is used in Spanish.

- An action that occurred and continues during an unfinished period of time.

   Example: <u>He leído</u>* doce libros este mes.
        <u>I have read</u> twelve books this month.

- An action in the past that happened during an unspecified period of time.

   Example: <u>Ha visitado</u> España también.
        <u>He has visited</u> Spain too.

- A repeated action that has occurred in the past but has a sense of immediacy because it is so recent.

   Example: <u>Hemos terminado</u> la tarea.
        <u>We've finished</u> the homework.

   * Present Perfect tense is underlined.

The Verb "Haber"

As stated above, the present perfect tense is formed with the auxiliary or "helping" verb "haber" in Spanish.

Haber- To have (auxiliary, helping, verb)

Yo	He	I have	Nosotros	Hemos	We have
Tú	Has	You have	Vosotros	Habéis	All of you have
Él, Ella, Usted (Ud.)	Ha	He, she has, you have	Ellos, Ustedes (Uds.)	Han	They, all of you have

Formation of the Present Perfect Tense

To form the present perfect tense, take a form of "haber" and add it to the past participle. The charts below will provide an example of the basic formation of an –ar verb and an -er or –ir verb in the present perfect tense.

Estudiar- To study

Yo	**He estudiado**	I have studied	Nosotros	**Hemos estudiado**	We have studied
Tú	**Has estudiado**	You have studied	Vosotros	**Habéis estudiado**	All of you have studied
Él, Ella, Usted (Ud.)	**Ha estudiado**	He, she has, you have studied	Ellos, Ustedes (Uds.)	**Han estudiado**	They have, all of you have studied

Venir- To come

Yo	**He venido**	I have come	Nosotros	**Hemos venido**	We have come
Tú	**Has venido**	You have come	Vosotros	**Habéis venido**	All of you have come
Él, Ella, Usted (Ud.)	**Ha venido**	He, she has, you have come	Ellos, Ustedes (Uds.)	**Han venido**	They have, all of you have come

■ DAY 2

OBJECTIVES

You will learn to:

- To state past action
- To state what someone has done
- To compare "haber" and "tener"

Present Perfect Tense (continued)

In the last section, you were introduced to the present perfect tense. In this section, you will learn more about the present perfect tense. Also, you will have more opportunity to form the present perfect tense as well as well as practice it by making sentences and asking questions.

Differences between "Haber" and "Tener"

In the last lesson, did you wonder why you couldn't use the verb "tener" to form the present perfect tense? Well, although "haber" and "tener" translate to be the same word in English, they are used very differently in Spanish. The points below will help to clarify the differences between the verbs.

HABER
- Is NOT used alone.
- Means "has" or "have."
- Is a helping verb.
- Is not used to show possession.
- Can NEVER take the place of "tener."

TENER
- Is used alone in a sentence.
- Means "has" or "have."
- Is NOT a helping verb.
- IS USED to show possession.
- Can NEVER take the place of "haber."

Examples:

He comprado la ropa.	I have bought the clothes.
Yo tengo la ropa.	I have the clothes.
Ha encontrado la moneda.	He has found the coins.
Tiene la moneda.	He has the coins.

The Past Participle in the Present Perfect Tense

In section 2.7, you learned that when the past participle is an adjective, it must agree with the noun it modifies. However, when the past participle is used to form a verb tense, it is no longer an adjective. Therefore, it does NOT need to agree with a noun. The past participle remains in the -ado or -ido form.

To review the formation of the past participle:

> Begin with the infinitive.
> Drop the -ar, -er, or -ir ending.
> Add -ado (to -ar verbs); add -ido (to -er and -ir verbs).

To form the present perfect tense, simply add a conjugated form of "haber" to the past participle.

Infinitive		Past Participle		Present Perfect Tense
Estar	→	Estado	→	He estado (I have been)
Ser	→	Sido	→	He sido (I have been)
Trabajar	→	Trabajado	→	Has trabajado (You have worked)
Conocer	→	Conocido	→	Ha conocido (You have known)
Dibujar	→	Dibujado	→	Hemos dibujado (We have drawn)
Tener	→	Tenido	→	Han tenido (They have had)

Peculiarities of the Past Participle

Sometimes a verb has a regular past participle for verb tenses and an irregular one used as an adjective (or noun). Here are some of the most common verbs that have irregular past participles.

Verb	Past Participle for... Present Perfect Tense	Past Participle for... Adjective
Despertar (To awaken)	Despertado	Despierto
Bendecir (To bless)	Bendecido	Bendito
Confundir (To confuse)	Confundido	Confuso
Suspender (To suspend)	Suspendido	Suspenso

 Nota Cultural

Las Molas

"Las molas" are layers of fabric that form works of art on the clothing of the Kuna people of Panama and Colombia. The fabric designs are made by layering colorful fabric. The layers of fabric are cut in intricate patterns. Each layer is cut slightly wider than the next so that every fabric layer is shown. The patterns chosen are typical of the natural habitat of the Kuna people; although, geometric patterns are also common. The word "mola" means "clothing" to the Kuna people. Although "molas" have a place in the Kuna society, in recent years they have become popular among tourists and have created a new economy for the Kuna people.

mola pattern

Kuna wearing mola pattern

Ejercicios

Exercise 2.8a:

Directions: In the paragraph, underline each occurrence of the present perfect tense.

Este mes, he viajado a México. He estado dos semanas en Cuernavaca. Mis amigos y yo nos hemos divertido mucho. Mis amigos y yo hemos visto muchos lugares preciosos. Hemos usado mucho la lengua de español durante mi visita. Voy a regresar a los lugares que he estado. Mis amigos, que me acompañaron, ya han regresado. He pensado en salir mañana, pero me faltan muchas cosas importantes tales como mi pasaporte y mi boleto de avión. Mi madre ha pagado por mi boleto de avión pero todavía no lo tengo. Tan pronto como tenerlo, me voy.

Exercise 2.8b:

Directions: Fill in the correct form of the auxiliary, helping, verb "haber."

1. Ellos _____ compartido muchas cosas.
2. Ella _____ leído los libros.
3. Yo _____ encontrado el dinero.
4. ¿_____ tú perdido algo?
5. Nosotros _____ lavado la ropa esta semana.
6. ¿_____ estado a Argentina, vosotros?
7. La vista (the view) _____ cambiado, ¿no?

Exercise 2.8c:

Directions: Translate the sentences above to English.

1. _____
2. _____
3. _____
4. _____
5. _____
6. _____
7. _____

Ejercicios

Exercise 2.8d:

Directions: Complete the charts to form the present perfect tense of the verbs.

Llegar – To Arrive

Yo	_____	I have arrived.	Nosotros	_____	We have arrived.
Tú	_____	You have arrived.	Vosotros	_____	All of you have arrived.
Él, Ella, Usted	_____	He/she has arrived. You have arrived.	Ellos, Ustedes	_____	They have arrived. All of you have arrived.

Vestir- To Dress

Yo	_____	I have dressed.	Nosotros	_____	We have dressed.
Tú	_____	You have dressed.	Vosotros	_____	All of you have dressed.
Él, Ella, Usted	_____	He/she has dressed. You have dressed.	Ellos, Ustedes	_____	They have dressed. All of you have dressed.

Exercise 2.8e:

Directions: Translate to Spanish.

1. We have not had the time.   _____

2. You have been a good friend.   _____

3. I have been to Costa Rica.   _____

4. She has worked this week.   _____

5. They have confused me.   _____
   (Place "me" in front of verb.)

Ejercicios

Exercise 2.8f:

Directions: Circle whether "haber" or "tener" would be used.

1. To show possession.   Haber   Tener

2. With the present perfect tense.   Haber   Tener

3. Used alone.   Haber   Tener

4. As an auxiliary verb.   Haber   Tener

5. To express age.   Haber   Tener

SECTION 2.9 - IRREGULAR PAST PARTICIPLES

■ DAY 1

OBJECTIVES

You will learn:
- To express past action
- To recognize irregular past participles
- To list irregular past participles

Irregular Past Participles

Although there are grammatical patterns to language, not all words follow these patterns at all times. Specifically, some verbs do not become past participles through the patterning taught in the last sections. These past participles will not end in -ado or -ido. In fact, there is no specific pattern for their formation. In turn, these past participles are formed irregularly and must be learned.

Irregular Past Participles

The infinitive in Spanish, its English meaning, and the past participle are included in the list below. The most common and widely used verbs form this first list; other irregular past participles will be included in the next lesson.

Infinitive	Meaning	Past Participle	Meaning
Abrir	to open	abierto	opened
Cubrir	to cover	cubierto	covered
Decir	to say, to tell	dicho	said, told
Describir	to describe	descri(p)to	described
Escribir	to write	escrito	written
Freír*	to fry	frito*	fried
Hacer	to do, to make	hecho	done, made
Imprimir*	to print	impreso*	printed
Ir	to go	ido	gone
Morir	to die	muerto	dead
Poner	to put, to place	puesto	put, placed
Resolver	to resolve	resuelto	resolved
Romper	to break	roto	broken
Satisfacer	to satisfy	satisfecho	satisfied
Ver	to see	visto	seen
Volver	to return	vuelto	returned

*Although uncommon in speech, "freído" and "imprimido" are also grammatically correct formations for the past participles.

■ Day 2

You will learn to:
- To define the terms "root word," "affix," "prefix," and "suffix"
- To recognize words from their roots
- To form regular and irregular past participles
- To form present perfect tense

Root Words

You are now at a good point in learning Spanish to discuss root words. A root word is the basic element from which the word has meaning. It is the foundation of the word. While some roots are words of their own (example: graph), others are not and need to be joined with affixes or other roots (example: rupt → interrupt, corrupt, etc.). Affixes are broken down into word strings that are attached in front of the root, known as a prefixes, and word strings that are attached after the root, known as suffixes.

It is important to learn about roots in Spanish for a couple of reasons.

1. Root words are often related in meaning.
2. Root words follow the same patterns.
3. Root words build vocabulary.

All parts of speech have root words. In discussing past participle formation and the present perfect tense, you have manipulated many verbs. Because many of these verbs are irregular, they do not follow the typical formation. By learning the root words for some irregular and regular verbs, you will be able to continue correct pattern formation while increasing your site word vocabulary.

Root	Meaning	Additional Verbs	Meaning
		Irregular in the Past Participle	
Abrir (Abierto)	To Open Reabrir	Entreabrir To reopen	To be ajar/half-open
Cubrir (Cubierto)	To cover	Descubrir Encubrir Recubrir	To discover To conceal To cover/coat
Escribir (Escrito)	To write (root = script) -scribe)	Describir Inscribir Prescribir Sobrescribir Suscribir Transcribir	To describe To inscribe/register To prescribe To overwrite To subscribe To transcribe

The next set is regular in the past participle. However, in future lessons, these verbs will be patterned together because of their root. It is important to recognize their roots.

Root	Meaning	Additional Verbs	Meaning
		Regular in the Past Participle	
Tener (Tenido)	To have	Abstener	To abstain
		Contener	To contain
		Detener	To detain/arrest/stop
		Mantener	To maintain/keep
		Obtener	To obtain/get
		Retener	To retain/hold back
		Sostener	To hold up/defend
-Ducir (not a verb) (-Ducido)	To lead (Latin origin)	Conducir	To drive
		Deducir	To guess/deduce
		Inducir	To induce
		Introducir	To introduce
		Producir	To produce
		Reducir	To reduce
		Traducir	To translate
-Struir (not a verb) (-struido)	To build	Construir	To construct
		Destruir	To destroy
		Instruir	To instruct
		Obstruir	To obstruct/block
		Reconstruir	To reconstruct

 Nota Cultural

What is "Yerba Mate"?

Yerba Mate is a traditional tea drink of the people in Argentina, Uruguay, Paraguay, and Brazil. Although Yerba Mate is a tea, it is also a social ritual and customary practice to the people of these countries.

To consume Yerba Mate, the leaves are first dried. They are placed in a hollowed out gourd often lined with silver (see below). Then, hot water is poured into the gourd. A bombilla (see below), a silver straw which strains the leaves, is used to drink the tea.

When the tea is finished, the gourd is refilled with hot water and passed to the next person in the group. It continues until the gourd makes it back to the server.

The Yerba Mate leaves are supposed to be extremely good for a person's health. Benefits of the Yerba Mate are known to be appetite control, detoxification, and rejuvenation, to name a few. In addition, the ritual is supposed to strengthen the bonds of friendship

Ejercicios

Exercise 2.9a:

Directions: Match the Spanish to the English.

1. _____ Vuelto   a. done
2. _____ Puesto   b. broken
3. _____ Roto   c. said
4. _____ Dicho   d. seen
5. _____ Visto   e. covered
6. _____ Cubierto   f. returned
7. _____ Hecho   g. put

Exercise 2.9b:

Directions: Fill in the correct past participle.

1. Geraldo ha sido _____ (dead) hace algún tiempo.
   Geraldo has been dead/murdered for some time.
2. No lo he _____ (seen).
   I have not seen it.
3. Han _____ (made) las camas.
   They have made the beds.
4. Hemos _____ (written) en nuestros cuadernos.
   We have written in our notebooks.
5. ¿Has _____ (printed) el trabajo?
   Have you printed the "job" (work)?

Exercise 2.9c:

Directions: Based on the picture and subject, write a sentence in the present perfect tense.

1.   Juanita   _____
                     _____
                     _____
                     _____
                     _____

2.   Julieta   _____
                     _____
                     _____
                     _____
                     _____

Ejercicios

3.  Xavier y Rosana _____
_____
_____
_____
_____

4.  Rogelio _____
_____
_____
_____
_____
_____

5. Mateo y Cataldo _____
_____
_____
_____
_____

Exercise 2.9d:

Directions: Circle the word that does NOT belong.

1.	Prescribir	Suscribir	Construir	Transcribir
2.	Reducir	Instruir	Obstruir	Reconstruir
3.	Tener	Contener	Haber	Mantener
4.	Reabrir	Cubrir	Entreabrir	Abrir
5.	Conducir	Traducir	Introducir	Destruir

6. Why don't the words circled belong? _____

Exercise 2.9e:

Directions: Choose the correct past participle for the present perfect tense.

1. Hacer a. Hacido b. Hecho
2. Resolver a. Resuelto b. Resolvido
3. Tener a. Techo b. Tenido
4. Venir a. Venido b. Vuelto
5. Descubrir a. Descubierto b. Descubrido
6. Escribir a. Escribido b. Escrito
7. Reabrir a. Reabierto b. Reabrido
8. Ir a. Ido b. Irido
9. Introducir a. Introducido b. Introducado
10. Reconstruir a. Reconstruado b. Reconstruido
11. Morir a. Morido b. Muerto
12. Poner a. Puesto b. Ponido
13. Romper a. Roto b. Rompido
14. Ver a. Vido b. Visto
15. Obstruir a. Obstruido b. Obstrusto

Ejercicios

Exercise 2.9f:

Directions: Translate the sentence to Spanish using the present perfect tense.

1. I have translated the Spanish.   _____

2. The girl has obtained the book.   _____

3. We have driven the car.   _____

4. They have already subscribed.   _____

5. Have you reopened the window?   _____

SECTION 2.10 - REVIEW OF UNIT 2

■ DAY 1

You will learn:
- To recall the first half of Unit II

| Review |

At the end of each unit you will review the main concepts in lessons 1-9. In addition, you will use lesson 10 to combine the concepts into one cohesive idea. Because each unit has a theme, the content of each lesson belongs with the other lessons of the unit. Lesson 10 provides the opportunity to combine all concepts to practice your proficiency.

The following outline lists the important concepts from each lesson. Go back to each lesson and review these concepts.

You should be able to explain the concept as well as use the concept in sentences and questions.

Spanish Review Outline

I. Lesson 1
A. List Classes
B. State and ask what classes you have

Use a form of "Tener" to express "have."

C. State and ask the time of the classes

¿A qué hora es la clase de _____?

La clase de _____ es a las _____.

II. Lesson 2
A. Describe Classes

Adjectives must agree in number and gender with the classes.

B. State what just happened

Acabar + de + infinitive = to have just _____

Acabo de comer. = I just ate.

III. Lesson 3
A. List Ordinal Numbers and their abbreviations

To abbreviate ordinal numbers:
     Do NOT use -st, -nd, -rd, etc. (1st, 2nd, 3rd, etc.)
     Instead, use –o or –a after the number (1°/1^{a}, 2°/2^{a}, 3°/3^{a})

B. List Transition words
C. Sequence Events

IV. Lesson 4
A. Name People at School
B. Address People with Titles
C. Express Favorites

Words for favorite = favorito/ preferido
               (must agree in number and gender with noun)

V. Lesson 5
A. List and Locate School Objects
B. List and Locate Classroom Objects

Use a form of "estar" to express location
"Hay" means "there is/are"

■ DAY 2

OBJECTIVES

You will learn to:

– Recall the second half of Unit II

Spanish Review Outline

VI. Lesson 6
A. State and Ask What is Missing/Lacking
B. Express "Need" another way

Me falta/n. = I am missing/lacking something/s.

VII. Lesson 7

A. List and Locate Rooms of a School
B. Describe using Past Participles

Start with the infinitive.
Drop the -ar, -er, or -ir ending.
Add -ado (for -ar verbs).
Add -ido (for -er or -ir verbs).

C. Recognize, Form, and Use Past Participles as Adjectives

Use the verb "estar."
The past participle must agree in number and gender
with the noun it modifies.

VIII. Lesson 8

A. Recognize, Form, and Use the Present Perfect Tense
B. Compare "Haber" and "Tener"

"Haber" and "Tener" are both verbs in Spanish that mean "to have."
However, "haber" is a helping verb that typically is NOT used alone.
"Tener" is used alone and is used to show possession.

C. Compare Past Participles Used as Adjectives and in Verb Tenses

At times, some verbs have two past participles: one that is used as an
adjective, and the other that is used for verb tenses.

IX. Lesson 9

A. Recognize, Form, and Use Irregular Past Participles
B. Recognize Root Words

A root is the foundation of the word. Knowing roots helps to follow
patterns, build vocabulary, and identify related words.

C. Pattern Past Participles and Verbs According to their Root Word

Culture Review Outline

In addition to the Spanish concepts, you also learned culture. Please review the culture concepts in this outline.

You should be able to explain each culture concept.

I. **Lesson 1**
- **School in Spain**
II. **Lesson 2**
-**Types of School in Spain**
III. **Lesson 3**
- **School Uniforms**
IV. **Lesson 4**
- **Grading Scale**
V. **Lesson 5**
- **Classrooms in Spanish-Speaking Countries**
VI. **Lesson 6**
- **Synonyms**
VII. **Lesson 7**
- **Expressions with Past Participles**
VIII. **Lesson 8**
- **Las Molas**
IX. **Lesson 9**
- **Yerba Mate**

Ejercicios

Exercise 2.10a:

Directions: Write a paragraph in Spanish about a Miguel's schedule. Include: class order, class descriptions, class names, and Miguel's teachers.

Order	Class	Description	Teacher
1st	Math	Favorite	Turka
2nd	Spanish	Interesting	Schipani Ortega
3rd	English	Easy	Modico
4th	Social Studies	Boring	Makellin
5th	Reading	Difficult	Jones

_____

_____

_____

_____

_____

_____

_____

_____

_____

_____

_____

_____

_____

_____

_____

_____

_____

_____

_____

Ejercicios

Exercise 2.10b:

Directions: Use the subject and the picture to create a sentence stating what just happened. Use "acabar + de + infinitive."

1. Juan

_____
_____
_____
_____

2. Roberto y Diana

_____
_____
_____
_____

3. I

_____
_____
_____
_____

4. We

_____
_____
_____
_____

5. You

_____
_____
_____
_____

Exercise 2.10c:

Directions: Build a sentence stating what item/s is/are missing in each room. Follow the example.

Example: *laboratory, we, desks*   En el laboratorio, nos faltan los pupitres.

    1. Classroom, they, pencils   _____
    2. Locker, I, book   _____
    3. Gym, he, clothes   _____
    4. Office, he, flag   _____
    5. Cafeteria, you, lunch/food   _____

Exercise 2.10d:

Directions: Answer the questions.

1. How do you form the past participle in Spanish?
2. How do you form the present perfect tense?
3. How can you use the past participle as an adjective?
4. What is a root word?
5. List 3 irregular past participles.

Section 2.6 _____ Date

Section 2.7 _____ Date

Section 2.8 _____ Date

Section 2.9 _____ Date

Section 2.10 _____ Date

Additional Notes _____ Date

FOOD

UNIT

3

SECTION 3.1 - FRUITS AND VEGETABLES

■ DAY 1

OBJECTIVES

You will learn:

- To identify fruits
- To list fruits

La Comida

La comida, or food, is the topic of Unit III. In this Unit, you will learn the names for all types of food: fruit, vegetables, protein, starches, fats and junk foods. Also, you will learn about the culture surrounding food and certain types of dishes specific to Hispanic and Latin American culture. Finally, you will be able to relate this information to breakfast, lunch, dinner, and restaurant scenarios. Let's get started!

Las Frutas - Fruits

La manzana	Apple
La banana	Banana
El plátano	Banana/plantain
La pera	Pear
El albaricoque	Apricot
El melocotón	Peach
La ciruela	Plum
El higo	Fig
La naranja	Orange
La toronja/ El pomelo	Grapefruit
La lima	Lime
El limón	Lemon
La piña	Pineapple
El coco	Coconut
La sandía	Watermelon
La cereza	Cherry
La fresa	Strawberry
La uva	Grape
La frambuesa	Raspberry
La mora	Blackberry
El arándano	Blueberry
El mango	Mango
La guava	Guava
La papaya	Papaya
El aguacate	Avocado
La oliva/ la aceituna	Olive
El tomate	Tomato

Fruit Stand in Barcelona

Review

To express a like or dislike use the verbs "gusta" or "gustan."

    Me gustan las manzanas.   I like apples.

    No me gustan los aguacates.   I do not like avocados.

To express that you do not like something "at all,"
place "nada" after a form of "gusta."

    No te gustan nada las olivas.   You do not like olives at all.

To express a "love" for something, use "encanta" or "encantan."

    Le encantan las uvas.   He loves grapes.

    No le encantan las toronjas.   He does not love grapefruit.

■ DAY 2

OBJECTIVES

You will learn to:
- To list classes at school
- To ask what classes others have and what they study

La Comida

In the last lesson, you learned the vocabulary for over twenty fruits. In this lesson, you will continue to build your vocabulary in Spanish while learning the name for a plentitude of vegetables.

Las Verduras/ Los Vegetales - Vegetables

La alcachofa	Artichoke
El espárrago	Asparagus
Los frijoles	Beans
La judías verdes	Green beans
La remolacha	Beet
El brócoli	Broccoli

Los coles de Bruselas	Brussels sprouts
La zanahoria	Carrot
La coliflor	Cauliflower
El apio	Celery
El chayote	Chayote
El garbanzo	Chickpea
El maíz	Corn
El choclo, el elote	Corn on the cob
El pepino	Cucumber
La berenjena	Eggplant
El ajo	Garlic
La lenteja	Lentil
La lechuga	Lettuce
La ensalada	Salad
El champiñón	Mushroom
La cebolla	Onion
El guisante	Pea
El pimiento	Pepper
La patata	Potato
La batata	Sweet potato/ yam
La calabaza	Pumpkin
El rábano	Radish
La espinaca	Spinach
El nabo	Turnip
El calabacín	Zucchini

 Nota Cultural

Nota Cultural: Las Frutas Tropicales, Tropical Fruits

Because many Spanish speaking countries are located in climates much warmer than North America, the produce is very different there as compared to here. In fact, many delicious and very nutritious fruits, which you've never heard of, grow in these countries.

The list below includes some of these tropical fruits and their pictures.

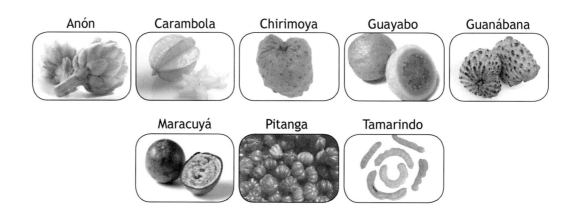

Anón   Carambola   Chirimoya   Guayabo   Guanábana

Maracuyá   Pitanga   Tamarindo

Ejercicios

Exercise 3.1a:

Directions: Write the name of the fruit under each picture. Make the word plural, if necessary.

Grapes	Avocado	Strawberry	Blueberry	Raspberry
_____	_____	_____	_____	_____

Lemon	Cherry	Peach	Pear	Blackberry
_____	_____	_____	_____	_____

Grapefruit	Watermelon	Orange	Pineapple	Apple
_____	_____	_____	_____	_____

Exercise 3.1b:

Directions: Fill in the missing letters. Then, give the name of the fruit in English. Follow the example.

Example: L __A__   c __l__ r __U__ e __L__ a = Plum

1. E ___   a l ___ a r i ___ o ___ ___ e = _____

2. ___ a   o ___ i ___ ___   = _____

3. ___ l   a ___ u a ___ ___ t ___   = _____

4. E l   ___ l ___ n ___ a ___ o   = _____

5. ___ l   ___ o ___ a ___ e   = _____

6. L ___   f ___ a ___ ___ u ___ s ___ = _____

7. E l   ___ o ___ o   = _____

8. E ___   m ___ ___ ___ o   = _____

9. L a   ___ u ___ ___ a   = _____

10. ___ a   p a ___ a ___ ___   = _____

Ejercicios

Exercise 3.1c:

Directions: Answer the questions in a full sentence in Spanish.

1. ¿Qué frutas te gustan?

   _____

2. ¿Qué frutas no te gustan?

   _____

3. ¿Te gustan las cerezas?

   _____

4. ¿Te gustan las frambuesas y las moras?

   _____

5. ¿Qué fruta te gusta más: la sandía o el coco?

   _____

6. ¿Qué fruta es tu favorita?

   _____

Exercise 3.1d:

Directions: Write the name of the vegetable under each picture. Make the word plural, if necessary.

Lettuce	Pepper	Potato	Cucumber	Mushroom
_____	_____	_____	_____	_____
Corn	Pumpkins	Artichokes	Carrots	Ear of Corn
_____	_____	_____	_____	_____
Radishes	Broccoli	Celery	Eggplant	Beans
_____	_____	_____	_____	_____

Exercise 3.1e:

Directions: Find the words in Spanish in the Word Search.

Garlic	Cauliflower	Chickpea	Zucchini	Spinach
Lentil	Brussels Sprout	Asparagus	Turnip	

K	C	I	W	O	N	C	K	K	V	M	P	A	C	D
B	O	W	O	Z	K	R	O	P	S	Z	C	W	W	W
B	L	F	I	N	C	M	O	U	B	A	W	Y	O	U
X	D	D	B	A	G	N	L	L	N	Z	C	F	S	U
K	E	Y	A	B	Q	Q	X	I	F	A	J	L	J	S
B	B	Z	U	R	K	M	P	N	L	I	C	V	K	Q
K	R	H	C	A	P	S	Q	A	Q	K	L	A	T	J
B	Ú	P	L	G	E	D	B	M	I	S	L	O	N	Z
O	C	Q	A	O	G	A	R	R	Á	P	S	E	C	A
J	E	N	S	L	C	C	D	Q	A	I	O	F	E	J
Q	L	U	A	Í	K	H	T	H	K	W	H	F	I	O
D	A	O	N	B	H	Q	Y	D	S	G	X	H	M	Q
T	S	U	Y	L	O	A	E	M	A	Y	W	P	M	M
L	E	N	T	E	J	A	V	D	V	X	L	U	L	H
O	Y	X	M	S	P	S	D	Y	R	P	G	I	O	C

Execise 3.1f:

Directions: Respond in a full sentence in Spanish.

1. ¿Qué prefieres: las frutas o los vegetales?

   _____

2. Identifica cinco verduras que comes normalmente y frecuentemente.

   _____

3. ¿Cuáles son los vegetales que no comes?

   _____

4. ¿Qué te gusta más: las patatas o las batatas?

   _____

5. ¿Tienes que comer las frutas y los vegetales durante las comidas completas en casa?

   _____

SECTION 3.2 - PROTEINS

■ DAY 1

You will learn to:

−To recognize proteins

−To list proteins

− To express how they would like meats prepared

Las Proteínas

This chapter will provide you with a list of food categorized as proteins. Proteins are foods rich in amino acids that are essential for cell growth and repair. Foods that are considered proteins can be meats, eggs, fishes, and proteins in the vegetarian form.

It is important to understand that in other cultures protein is a large part of each meal and snacks. In Latin American countries and Spain, the vegetarian moment has not gained as much popularity as it has in the United States.

Furthermore, the types of protein eaten in each country vary according to the natural resources of that country. For example, because Argentina has plenty of cattle, Argentineans will eat more red meat than the people of Cuba. Because Spain is located on a peninsula, Spaniards diets are full of fish and seafood.

The list of protein will be broken down into two days due to the large amount of vocabulary related to this topic. In addition, the proteins are so categorized by types so related words can be acquired together.

Las proteínas - Proteins

La carne (de res)	("Red") Meat
El bistec	Steak
El filete	Fillet
La hamburguesa	Hamburger
La ternera	Veal
El pastel de carne	Meatloaf
El caldo de <u>conejo</u>	<u>Rabbit</u> stew
La carne de cerdo	Pork
El lomo	Pork loin
La chuleta	(Pork) chop
La salchicha	Sausage
El jamón	Ham
El chorizo	Spanish-style salami
El tocino	Bacon
El perrito caliente	Hotdog

La carne de ave	Poultry
El pollo	Chicken
La pechuga	Breast
La alita	Wing
El huevo	Egg
El pavo	Turkey
El pato	Duck

Related Vocabulary

Casi crudo	Rare
Poco hecho	
Término medio	Medium
En su punto	
Bien cocido	Well-done
Muy hecho	
A la parrilla	Grilled
Al horno	Baked
Frito/a	Fried
Asado/a	Roasted
La carne asada	Barbecued meat
Una carne asada	A barbecue
Una barbacoa	A barbecue

Examples:

Quisiera* el pollo a la parilla.

    I would like* the chicken grilled.

Me gustaría* el bistec casi crudo.

    I would like* the steak rare.

Me encantan las alitas.

    I love chicken wings.

No me gusta nada el jamón.

    I do not like ham at all.

La carne asada y el pollo asado son mis favoritos.

    Barbecued meat and roasted chicken are my favorites.

■ DAY 2

You will learn to:

- ‒ To list proteins
- ‒ To categorize protiens
- ‒ To express their food preference

▌ Las proteínas (Continuación) ▌

In the last section, you learned roughly one-half of the list of proteins. You will continue to acquire vocabulary in this lesson as you move from the land-based and traditional protein sources towards other sources.

El pescado	**Fish**
El salmón	Salmon
El bacalao	Cod
El atún	Tuna
El marisco	**Seafood, Shellfish**
La langosta	Lobster
El langostino	Prawn
El camarón	Shrimp
La gamba	Shrimp
El cangrejo	Crab
La almeja	Clam
El mejillón	Mussel
La ostra	Oyster
La vieira	Scallop
El calamar	Squid
El pulpo	Octopus
Los Platos Vegetarianos	**Vegetarian Dishes**
Las legumbres	Legumes
Los frijoles	Beans
Las nueces	Nuts
La crema de cacahuete	Peanut butter
Las semillas	Seeds
La soja	Soy
Related Vocabulary	
El vegetariano	Vegetarian
El carnívoro	Meat-eater

Example

Porque soy vegetariano, prefiero comer los platos vegetarianos.

Because I am vegetarian, I prefer to eat vegetarian dishes.

Los carnívoros comen mucha carne de res y carne de cerdo.

Meat-eaters eat a lot of "red" meat and pork.

Los mariscos incluyen los camarones, los langostinos, los cangrejos y las langostas.

Shellfish includes shrimp, prawn, crab, and lobster.

Nota Cultural

What is "Chorizo"?

Chorizo is cured pork. It is an extremely popular and a regularly eaten food in Spain. Chorizo has a red color due to the paprika flavoring. It comes in sweet or spicy varieties. Chorizo can be eaten for breakfast, lunch, dinner, or as a snack. You can make sandwiches with chorizo, place it on crusty bread, eat it with eggs, or simply slice and chew. It is worth a trip to Spain just to eat delicious chorizo!

Ejercicios

Exercise 3.2a:

Directions: Draw a picture of the vocabulary word.

1. El pastel de carne   2. Los huevos y tocino   3. El pollo frito

4. Una hamburguesa   5. Las salchichas   6. El caldo de conejo
   y dos perritos caliente

Exercise 3.2b:

Directions: Circle which meat you prefer.

1. Prefiero...

   el pollo asado   el pollo frito   el pollo al horno

2. Prefiero...

   la carne de res   la carne de cerdo   la carne de ave

3. Prefiero...

   el filete   la chuleta   el lomo

4. Prefiero...

   la carne poco hecho   la carne en su punto   la carne muy hecho

5. Prefiero los huevos con...

   salchicha   jamón   tocino

Exercise 3.2c:

Directions: Translate it to Spanish.

1. I would like the fillet medium-well.   _____
2. I like veal.   _____
3. I don't like eggs.   _____
4. I would like a Spanish-style salami sandwich.   _____
5. I don't like pork at all.   _____

Exercise 3.2d:

Directions: Circle which three belong.

1. Los Mariscos
    a. el bacalao   b. las gambas   c. el pulpo   d. las almejas

2. La Carne de Res
    a. el filete   b. el bistec   c. las legumbres   d. la hamburguesa

3. El Pescado
    a. el salmón   b. el atún   c. el bacalao   d. la langosta

4. La Carne de Cerdo
    a. las chuletas   b. la soja   c. el lomo   d. el tocino

5. La Carne de Ave
    a. el pato   b. el pavo   c. la ostra   d. el pollo

6. Los Platos Vegetarianos
    a. la vieira   b. las nueces   c. las semillas   d. la crema de cacahuete

Ejercicios

Exercise 3.2e:

Directions: Match the Spanish and English.

1. ____ el atún   a. lobster
2. ____ los legumbres   b. peanut butter
3. ____ la crema de cacahuete   c. tuna
4. ____ el marisco   d. nuts
5. ____ los calamares   e. shrimp
6. ____ el pescado   f. cod
7. ____ las nueces   g. squid
8. ____ el bacalao   h. legumes
9. ____ la langosta   i. seafood
10. ____ los camarones   j. fish

Exercise 3.2f:

Directions: List three proteins in each category.

Los pescados   **Las Carnes de Res**   **Las Carnes de Ave**

_____   _____   _____
_____   _____   _____
_____   _____   _____

Los Platos Vegetarianos   **Las Carnes de Cerdo**   **Los Mariscos**

_____   _____   _____
_____   _____   _____
_____   _____   _____

SECTION 3.3 - CARBOHYDRATES AND DESSERTS

■ DAY 1

You will learn:

‑ To list carbohydrates

Los carbohidratos

Carbohydrates are the starches in our diets. Carbohydrates come in many forms, some better for you than others. In this section, you will learn about carbohydrates that are thought to comprise meals. In the next and subsequent sections, you will learn about carbohydrates eaten as snacks, sweets, or junk food.

Los carbohidratos

El pan	Bread
El pan tostado	Toast
El panecillo	Bun
La tortilla	Tortilla (Mexican)
La pasta	Pasta
Los espaguetis	Spaghetti
El arroz	Rice
El cereal	Cereal
La harina de avena	Oatmeal
La patata	Potato
El puré de patata	Mashed potato
Las patatas fritas	French fries
La batata	Sweet potato/yam
La pizza	Pizza
La harina	Flour
Integral	Whole grain
El trigo	Wheat

Related Vocabulary

La dieta baja en carbohidratos	Low-carb diet
Una rebanada de pan	A slice of bread
Una porción de pizza	A slice of pizza

■ DAY 2

You will learn:
- To list sweets

Los Postres

Carbohydrates also include the sticky, gooey, stuff everyone loves. In this section, you will learn vocabulary for some of the more common sweets.

Los Postres

Los dulces	Sweets
El caramelo	Hard candy
Los chupa-chups	Lollipops
La comida basura	Junk food
El pastel	Cake (with filling and icing)
La torta	Cake (with filling and icing)
El queque	Cake (no filling, with or without icing)
La tarta	Pie, tart
Las galletas	Cookies
Las galletas de María	María cookies (discus-shaped, graham type cookie)
Las galletas saladas	Crackers
El bizcocho	Sweet bread (danish, cinnamon roll, etc.)
Los barquillos	Wafers, cones, waffles
El bollo	Roll, muffin
Los panqueques	Pancakes

Related Vocabulary

El jarabe de arce	Maple syrup
El glaseado	Icing
...de chocolate	Chocolate
...de vainilla	Vanilla

Nota Cultural

Las Magdalenas

Magdalenas are muffins, or little breads, that are eaten for breakfast or as a snack, during the day. Magdalenas are deliciously flavored with lemon, or orange zest, and typically made with olive oil. They can be homemade, bought at a bakery, or sold in stores.

Ejercicios

Exercise 3.3a:

Directions: Write the Spanish vocabulary word on the line.

Rice   1.   _____

Bun   2.   _____

Tortilla   3.   _____

French Fries   4.   _____

Spaghetti   5.   _____

Exercise 3.3b:

Directions: Fill in the boxes with vocabulary from your list.

Normalmente, como….	Nunca como…

Ejercicios

Exercise 3.3c:

Directions: Answer the questions in Spanish.

1. Describe tu pizza favorita.
2. ¿Con qué frecuencia comes los carbohidratos?
3. ¿Cuándo comes el pan tostado, cuántas rebanadas comes?
4. ¿Qué prefieres: las patatas asadas o el puré de patatas?
5. ¿Qué comen los italianos?

Exercise 3.3d:

Directions: Fill-in the answers to the crossword puzzle.

Across

1. Hard candy
3. Sweets

Down

1. Junk food
2. Cake
4. Lollipops

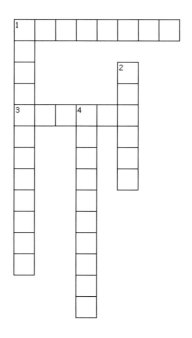

Ejercicios

Exercise 3.3e:

Directions: Write a small paragraph about the items in the pictures. Begin with, "In the picture, there is/are...."

_____

_____

_____

_____

_____

_____

_____

_____

_____

_____

SECTION 3.4 - DAIRY AND SNACKS

■ DAY 1

OBJECTIVES

You will learn:
- To list dairy products

Dairy Products

Dairy products are products made from milk. In this lesson, you will learn vocabulary for foods and drinks that are milk based.

Los Productos Lácteos- Dairy Products

La leche	Milk
El yogur	Yogurt
El queso	Cheese
El queso de untar (Spain)	Cream cheese
El queso cremoso (Mexico)	Cream cheese
La nata	Cream
La nata montada	Whipped cream
El helado	Ice cream
El sorbete de leche	Ice milk
El batido	Milk shake
El licuado	Smoothie
El pudín	Pudding
El arroz con leche	Rice pudding
El flan	Flan
La mantequilla	Butter
La margarina	Margarine

Related Vocabulary

La leche entera	Whole milk
La leche desnatada	Skim milk
La leche semi-desnatada	2% milk
La leche con chocolate	Chocolate milk
La leche en polvo	Powerdered (dry) milk

The Verb "Preferir"

If you want to express your preferences, you can use the verb "preferir" which means "to prefer." The verb is stem changing, so it changes from "e" to "ie" in all of the forms except for "nosotros" and "vosotros."

Preferir - To Prefer

Yo	Prefiero	I prefer	Nosotros	Preferimos	We prefer
Tú	Prefieres	You prefer	Vosotros	Preferís	All of you prefer
Él, Ella Usted (Ud.)	Prefiere	He, she prefers You (formal)	Ellos, Ustedes (Uds.)	Prefieren	They prefer All of you

■ DAY 2

OBJECTIVES

You will learn to:
– To identify snacks

Snacks

Snacks are things you eat in between meals. Snacking varies by country. The actual word "snack" also varies among people of different countries. In this section, you will learn all about snacks.

Snacks

The three basic words for snacks are the following:

Los tentempiés – used mostly in Spain
Las meriendas – used everywhere
Las botanas – used mostly in Mexico

Types of Snacks

El bocadillo	Sandwich
El sándwich	Sandwich
El queso	Cheese
Las olivas/ las aceitunas	Olives
Las patatas fritas	Potato Chips
La fruta	Fruit
La fruta seca	Dried Fruit
Las nueces	Nuts
Las palomitas	Popcorn
El chocolate	Chocolate
La chocolatina	Candy Bar
La paleta helada	Popsicle

What happened to pretzels?

In Spain, and other Spanish-speaking countries, pretzels do not exist. You may see a pretzel as an imported food, but, for the most part, pretzels are not a food eaten in Spanish-speaking countries. In fact, because snacking varies culturally, many of the snacks we have in the U.S. are unheard of in Spanish-speaking countries.

Related Vocabulary

Picar	To snack
Tomar una merienda	To have a snack
Coger algo de picar	To choose something to snack on

Examples

Voy a picar.
    I am going to snack.

Tomo una merienda casi todos los días.
    I have a snack almost every day.

Quiero coger algo de picar.
    I want to choose something to snack on.

Nota Cultural

Goat's Milk

I bet you would never think of drinking goat's milk or eating cheese made from goat's milk. But, in many parts of the world, including Spanish-speaking countries, goat's milk is preferred to cow's milk. Goat's milk is believed to be more digestible than cow's milk and it contains less lactose than cow's milk.

Ejercicios

Exercise 3.4a:

Directions: Categorize the dairy products by the two choices.

      A. Se bebe (One drinks...)   B. Se come (One eats...)

1. ____ el arroz con leche.
2. ____ la leche.
3. ____ el flan.
4. ____ el pudín.
5. ____ el batido.
6. ____ el yogur.
7. ____ el queso.
8. ____ el queso de nata.
9. ____ el licuado.
10. ____ la leche chocolateada.

Ejercicios

Exercise 3.4b:

Directions: Choose your preference; then, write a sentence in Spanish stating your preference.

¿Qué prefieres?

Los licuados o
Los batidos

_____

¿Qué prefieres?

El helado o
El sorbete de leche

_____

¿Qué prefieres?

El pudín o
El arroz con leche

_____

¿Qué prefieres?

La margarina o
La mantequilla

_____

¿Qué prefieres?

La leche o
La leche con chocolate

_____

¿Qué prefieres?

La leche entera o
La leche desnatada

_____

Exercise 3.4c:

Directions: Fill in the correct form of "preferir."

1. Yo _____ beber la leche.

2. ¿Qué _____ tú?

3. Mi hermano _____ la leche con chocolate.

4. Mis abuelos _____ el arroz con leche.

5. Nosotros _____ cosas vegetarianas.

Exercise 3.4d:

Directions: Write the vocabulary word in Spanish.

1.

Popcorn

_____

2.

Dried Fruit

_____

3.

Cheese

_____

4.

Olives

_____

5.

Popsicle

_____

6.

Chocolate Candy Bar

_____

Exercise 3.4e:

Directions: Translate it to Spanish.

1. My favorite snacks are dried fruit and nuts.

_____

2. On what are you going to snack?

_____

3. I am going to have a snack.

_____

4. I am choosing popcorn to snack on.

_____

5. I love to eat popsicles.

_____

SECTION 3.5 - CONDIMENTS AND DRINKS

■ DAY 1

OBJECTIVES

You will learn:
- To list condiments

Los condimentos

Most people would agree that food just doesn't taste the same without certain condiments. A hotdog wouldn't be a hotdog without ketchup and mustard. A salad just wouldn't have any take without dressing. In this section, you will learn the vocabulary in Spanish for condiments.

Los condimentos

La sal	Salt
La pimienta	Pepper
Negra/blanca	Black/white
La salsa de tomate	Ketchup
El ketchup	Ketchup
La mostaza	Mustard
La mostaza francesa	French Mustard
El azúcar	Sugar
El aderezo para ensaladas	Salad Dressing
El aliño	Dressing
El aceite de oliva	Oil
El vinagre	Vinegar
La mayonesa	Mayonnaise
La salsa picante	Hot sauce
Pico de gallo	Freshly diced vegetables with seasonings
La salsa	Sauce, any kind

Examples:

Prefiero sazonar la comida con la sal y la pimienta.
> I prefer to season the food with salt and pepper.

Bebo el té sin azúcar.
> I drink tea without sugar.

Se usa el aliño con las ensaladas.
> Dressing is used with salads.

■ DAY 2

You will learn to:

– To list drinks

Las Bebidas

What are some things you drink? Are you a Starbucks® person? Or, maybe you don't like coffee. In this section, you will learn the vocabulary for drink names.

Las Bebidas

El agua	Water
Con hielo	With ice
El agua con gas	Club soda
El gaseoso	Carbonated water
El refresco	Soda
La coca-cola	Coke
La coca-cola de dieta	Diet Coke
(or Coca-Cola light)	
El jugo	Juice
El jugo de naranja	Orange juice
La bebida deportiva	Sports Drink
El café	Coffee
El café con leche	Coffee with milk
El té	Te
El té helado	Iced tea
El té frío	Iced tea
La limonada	Lemonade
El chocolate	Hot chocolate
El vino	Wine
El vino tinto	Red wine
El vino blanco	White wine
La cerveza	Beer
El alcohol	Alcohol
Sin alcohol	Without Alcohol

Nota Cultural

Los Churros con El Chocolate

"Churros" and "chocolate" are eaten in Spain for breakfast or as a snack.
"Churros" are long fried doughnut tubes. They are covered in cinnamon and sugar. Sometimes they are even filled with different creams or chocolate.
"Chocolate" is a very rich hot chocolate. It is different from the hot chocolate we know in the U.S. because it is much thicker and made from better quality chocolate.

Ejercicios

Exercise 3.5a:

Directions: On the line, write the condiments that would possibly accompany the food.

1. El perrito caliente   _____

2. Las alitas   _____

3. La lechuga y los tomates   _____

4. El atún   _____

5. Los chips   _____

Ejercicios

Exercise 3.5b:

Directions: Unscramble the words to reveal one of your vocabulary words.

1. Vinegar   NIGVERA   ☐☐☐☐☐☐ (4)

2. Pepper   ITMAPNIE   ☐☐☐☐☐☐☐ (6)

3. Mustard   ZOAMAST   ☐☐☐☐☐☐ (5)

4. Salt   LAS   ☐☐☐

5. Mayonnaise   NOYSEMAA   ☐☐☐☐☐☐☐ (1)

6. Olive Oil   EECOEDAILIAVT   ☐☐☐☐☐☐☐☐☐☐☐ (3) (2)

☐F☐☐☐☐ (1 2 3)   ☐☐ (4 5)   F U ☐ (6)

Exercise 3.5c:

Directions: Create the questions in Spanish.

1. Do you drink iced tea?   _____

2. How often do you drink soda?   _____

3. Do you use sugar in coffee?   _____

4. What do you prefer: coke or diet coke? _____

5. Do you like churros and chocolate?   _____

Exercise 3.5d:

Directions: Answer the questions in full sentences in Spanish.

1. _____

2. _____

3. _____

4. _____

5. _____

NOTES

Section 3.1 _____ Date

Section 3.2 _____ Date

Section 3.3 _____ Date

Section 3.4 _____ Date

Section 3.5 _____ Date

Additional Notes _____ Date

SECTION 3.6 - DESCRIBING FOOD

■ DAY 1

OBJECTIVES

You will learn:
- To list adjectives to describe food
- To describe food

Adjectives to Describe Food

In this section, you will learn how to describe the food you eat.

Adjectives to Describe Food

Amargo	Bitter, sour
Agrio	Sour
Dulce	Sweet
Azucarado	Sugary/ sweet
Salado	Salty
Picante	Hot, spicy
Mantecoso	Buttery
Sabroso	Tasty
Delicioso	Delicious
Rico	Rich
Soso	Bland
Sin sabor	Without flavor/taste

Regarding Temperature

Use these adjectives with the verb "estar" for the most part.

Caliente	Hot
Tibio	Warm
Frío	Cold

Phrases with Food

¡Qué asco!	How awful!
¡Qué rico!	How delicious!

Adjective Agreement

As a reminder, adjectives must agree in number and gender with the nouns they describe. Nouns can be masculine or feminine, singular or plural.

El postre es sabroso.   (masculine singular)

Los postres son sabrosos. (masculine plural)

La torta es sabrosa. (feminine singular)

Las tortas son sabrosas. (feminine plural)

If you need to review noun and adjective agreement, please refer to Unit III of Part I.

Ser and Estar

You are already very familiar with the verbs "ser" and "estar." Because both words translate to mean "is, am" or "are," sometimes it is difficult to tell when to use which verb.

With foods, it is appropriate to use both. However, to use them correctly, keep this simple rule in mind.

When describing the characteristics of the food, use "ser."

When describing the condition of the food, use "estar."

In Spanish 2, you will learn, in more detail, the differences. But for now, this is a simple way to distinguish between the two verbs.

Examples:

La salsa es muy picante.

La salsa está muy picante.

The first sentence means that the sauce is normally very hot/spicy. "Very hot/spicy" is a characteristic of the sauce.

The second sentence means that the sauce is not normally hot/spicy, but it is now. Although the sauce would normally not be described as hot/spicy, its condition is hot/spicy now. Remember that estar is used to describe temporary conditions.

■ DAY 2

You will learn to:
- To say "very" or "extremely" with adjectives

Adjectives Ending in "-ísimo"

As you already learned the word "muy" means "very" in Spanish. It is placed in front of the adjective. However, there is another way to express "very" in Spanish. You can add the correct form of "-ísimo" to the end of an adjective. When added to the end of an adjective it conveys the meaning of "very" or "extremely." If added to the end of an adjective, do not place "muy" in front of the adjective.

Adjective Formation

- For an adjective ending in a vowel, drop the vowel
  and add the appropriate form of -ísimo.

  -ísimo   -ísima   -ísimos   -ísimas

- For an adjective ending in a consonant, add the appropriate form of -ísimo.

- For an adjective ending in -co, -ca, -cos, or -cas, there is a spelling
  change. You have to <u>change the -c to -qu.</u> Then, the -o, -a, -os,
  or -as is dropped. The appropriate form of -ísimo is added.

Examples:

Mucho → muchísimo
  A lot → extremely

Guapa → guapísima
  Good looking → extremely/very good looking

Sabrosos → sabrosísimos
  Tasty → extremely/very tasty

Fácil → facilísimo
  Easy → extremely/very easy

Ricas → riquísimas
  Rich → extremely/ very rich

In Sentences

Cuesta muchísimo dinero.

> It costs an extreme amount of money.

La chica es guapísima.

> The girl is extremely good looking.

Los panqueques son sabrosísimos.

> The pancakes are very tasty.

El examen es facilísimo.

> The test is really easy.

Las tartas son riquísimas.

> The pies/tarts are extremely rich.

 Nota Cultural

El chocolate

Did you ever wonder where chocolate came from, and when? Did you know that Native Americans were the first recorded people to grow and use chocolate? In fact, the Mayans elite society was only allowed to consume chocolate, called "xocalatl," which was an unsweetened and bitter drink. The drink became so popular that the Mayan people had cocoa plantations in the Yucatan peninsula. They also began to tax the drink. Explorers for Spain, like Christopher Columbus and Hernán Cortez, encountered the drink. Spaniards were the first to sweeten the drink with sugar and add flavorings like vanilla to enhance the taste of chocolate.

Ejercicios

Exercise 3.6a:

Fill in the correct adjective.

1. Las galletas saladas son _____.

2. Las galletas son _____.

3. El limón es _____.

4. El agua no tiene _____.

5. Los pimientos son _____.

Exercise 3.6b:

Directions: Translate it to Spanish.

1. The water is warm.   _____

2. The mashed potatoes are bland.   _____

3. The popcorn is buttery.   _____

4. The tea is cold.   _____

5. The beef is very tasty.   _____

Exercise 3.6c:

Directions: Circle the appropriate reaction.

1. La crema está amarga.   ¡Qué asco!   ¡Qué rico!

2. El pollo está azucarado.   ¡Qué asco!   ¡Qué rico!

3. La comida está muy deliciosa.   ¡Qué asco!   ¡Qué rico!

4. Los caramelos son picantes.   ¡Qué asco!   ¡Qué rico!

5. Porque no tiene sabor, el yogur es soso.   ¡Qué asco!   ¡Qué rico!

Exercise 3.6d:

Directions: Change the sentence so the adjective ends in the correct form of -ísimo.

1. La clase es muy interesante.   _____

2. La comida es muy rica.   _____

3. Las chicas son muy buenas.   _____

4. Los churros son muy sabrosos.   _____

SECTION 3.7 - EXPRESSIONS WITH FOOD

■ DAY 1

OBJECTIVES

You will learn:

⁻ To state and ask about hunger and thirst

⁻ To use expressions with food

To Be Hungry or Thirsty

There are two expressions in Spanish to express hunger or thirst. The expressions use the verb "tener" which means "to have." Although you already know this verb, you will have a chance to review it in this section with the expressions.

| Tener hambre | To be hungry |
| Tener sed | To be thirsty |

Review of Tener

Yo	tengo	= I have	Nosotros Nosotras	tenemos	= we have
Tú	tienes	= you have	Vosotros Vosotras	tenéis	= all of you have
Él Ella	tiene	= he/she has	Ellos Ellas	tienen	= they have
Usted (Ud.)	tiene	= you (formal) have	Ustedes (Uds.)	tienen	= all of you have

Examples:

¿Tienes hambre?	Are you hungry?
¿Tienes sed?	Are you thirsty?
No, no tengo hambre.	No, I am not hungry.
Acabamos de comer.	We just ate.
Pero, ella tiene sed.	But, she is thirsty.

Other Food Expressions

Other expressions used with food are listed below. These expressions all use a form of the verb "comer," "to eat."

¿Qué hay de comer?	What's there to eat?
Comer como una vaca*	To eat a ton (literally, to eat "like a cow")
Comer fuerte	To eat a big meal
Ser de buen comer	To enjoy one's food

*This expression is informal and should be used only among friends, family and in other casual settings.

Examples:

Tengo mucha hambre; voy a comer fuerte.
> I am really hungry; I am going to eat a big meal.

Después de hacer ejercicios, siempre come fuerte.
> After exercising, he always eats a big meal.

Soy de buen comer, cuando no preparo la comida.
> I enjoy my food when I don't make the meal.

■ DAY 1

OBJECTIVES

You will learn to:
- To choose appropriate breakfast, lunch, and dinner choices
- To use food expressions in breakfast, lunch, and dinner scenarios

Breakfast, Lunch, and Dinner

Although you know vocabulary for hundreds of foods and drinks, you have not yet put the vocabulary together to make meals. In this section, you will separate food into categories and create meals reflecting typical breakfasts, lunches, and dinners.

Las Comidas – Meals

El desayuno	Breakfast
El almuerzo/la comida*	Lunch
La cena	Dinner
La merienda	Late- afternoon snack

En…	At…
Para…	For…

*In most Spanish-speaking countries, el almuerzo means "lunch." In Spain, however, la comida is the word for lunch, and el almuerzo refers to a late morning snack (often coffee and some type of bread or small sandwich) eaten around 11am.

Los Verbos- Verbs

Desayunar	To eat breakfast
Almorzar	To eat lunch (stem changing o → ue)
Comer	To eat lunch (in Spain)
Merendar	To have an afternoon snack (stem changing e → ie)
Cenar	To eat dinner

Examples:

En el desayuno, hay huevos con queso y tocino.

> At breakfast, there are eggs with cheese and bacon.

Para el almuerzo, comemos los sándwiches de jamón y bebemos los refrescos.

> For lunch, we eat ham sándwiches and drink soda.

Cenamos a las 7:00 de la tarde.

> We eat dinner at 7 p.m.

Nota Cultural

National Dishes in Costa Rica

If you ever get a chance to visit Costa Rica you'll have to try "gallo pinto" and "casado."

"Gallo Pinto" translates to "spotted rooster." The seasoned mixture of rice and beans is served for breakfast. Often sour cream is served on the side. In addition, you can eat eggs and a side of bacon or sausage with "gallo pinto."

"Casado" translates to "married." "Casado" consists of white rice, black or red beans served with pork, steak, or chicken, a small portion of cabbage/lettuce & tomato salad, and fried plantains. "Casado" is served for lunch/dinner.

Ejercicios

Exercise 3.7a:

Directions: Fill in the missing word in Spanish.

1. Acabo de comer 4 hamburguesas; como como una _____.

2. Voy a comer porque _____ mucha hambre.

3. Soy de _____ comer.

4. Bebo el agua porque tengo _____.

5. ¿Qué _____ de comer?

Exercise 3.7b:

Directions: Write a sentence in Spanish appropriate for the given situation.

1. She is dying of hunger.   _____

2. I have a big appetite.   _____

3. He wants to know what there is to eat. _____

4. It appears that she is licking her spoon. _____

5. They are really thirsty.   _____

Ejercicios

Exercise 3.7c:

Directions: Draw at least 3 foods on the plate for each meal. Label the foods in Spanish.

El Desayuno   El Almuerzo   La Cena

      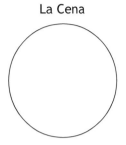

Exercise 3.7d:

Directions: Choose which meal it would be.

   A. Para el desayuno….   B. Para el almuerzo…   C. Para la cena…

1. _____ Como el casado todos los días.
2. _____ Tengo un sándwich de queso y tomate con unos chips.
3. _____ Me gusta comer las magdalenas.
4. _____ Por las mañanas, como el yogur con fresas y el cereal.
5. _____ Mi madre prepara unos filetes, batatas, y judías verdes.

Exercise 3.7e:

Directions: Based on the plate of food, write a sentence. Include whether the meal is for: breakfast, lunch, or dinner.

_____

_____

_____

SECTION 3.8 - PLACE SETTING; SPANISH FOOD VERSUS MEXICAN FOOD

■ DAY 1

OBJECTIVES

You will learn:

– To set the table
– To list place settings

Place Settting

In this lesson you will learn the vocabulary for basic place settings in Spanish as well as the proper placement of utensils.

Los Utensilios- Utensils

El tenedor	Fork
El cuchillo	Knife
La cuchara	Spoon
El vaso	Glass
La taza	Cup
El platillo	Saucer
El tazón	Bowl
El plato	Plate
La servilleta	Napkin

Review

To say the use of a utensil:

Se usa el cuchillo para cortar la carne.

To say that you are missing a utensil:

Me falta la servilleta.

To say you need to set the table.

Necesito poner la mesa.

To say the placement of a utensil.

La cuchara está a la derecha del cuchillo.

■ Day 2

OBJECTIVES

You will learn to:
- To list Spanish food
- To list Mexican food
- To compare Spanish and Mexican food
- To demonstrate an understanding of mealtimes

Spanish Food versus Mexican Food

For someone who is unfamiliar with the different cultures of Spanish-speakers, it may be difficult to compare food from Spain and from Mexico. There are some very distinct differences as well as some similarities.

Spanish Food and Meals

Breakfast is not much of a meal, but a bite to eat. It is typical for Spaniards to have coffee, café con leche, or chocolate with María cookies, Magdalena muffins or toast.

The main meal of the day- la comida- is served around 2 p.m. The meal typically has three courses: soup or salad, the meat platter accompanied with fresh crusty bread and a vegetable, and fruit or dessert. It is also common to serve wine with this meal. Paella is a national dish to Spain and typically served for the main meal on Sunday.

The last meal of the day- la cena- is normally served from 9 p.m. to 11 p.m. It is lighter meal that consists of soup with fresh crusty bread, in addition to tortilla española/patata, eggs with french fries, or croquetas. In between la comida and la cena, it is common to have a small snack or merienda between 6 and 8 pm.

Often, Spanairds do not eat the last meal of the day at home. Instead, they will go for to a bar or restaurant to have "tapas." Tapas are small portions of appetizer style food. A list of common tapas includes: calamares (squid), aceitunas (olives), queso con anchoa (cheese with anchovies), albóndigas (meatballs), chorizo (Spanish-style sausage), gambas (shrimp), patatas bravas (seasoned potatoes), tortilla española (Spanish-style omelet), or croquetas (croquettes). There are other "tapas," but these are the most common.

Where are the "tortillas"?

Tortillas in Spain are omelets or frittatas. The round flat-bread that you know does not exist in Spanish cuisine. The round flat-bread known as "tortilla" is part of the Mexican and Latin diet.

Mexican Food and Meals

Breakfast is also not much of a meal in Mexico either. Coffee, hot chocolate or atole (a thick hot drink that is made with corn, rice or oats) is served with cereal, sweet bread, fruit, or yogurt (sometimes with granola).

Sometime during the morning there is also a snack. A snack consists of drinkable yogurt, or tortilla that includes avocado, chicken, or ham. Nuts or bite-sized treats are also common snacks.

The main meal of the day is also lunch. The meal also has several courses, including soup or salad, a main dish, and dessert. The main dish could be a meat, vegetable, and tortillas or it can be one of the more traditional dishes of Mexico. Some of those dishes are: mole poblano (unique sauce and chicken), tamales, enchiladas, flautas, chilaquiles, chimichangas, and empanadas.

The last meal of the day is also very light and can consist of soup, a tortilla sandwich or a tostada.

Examples of Spanish Food

Paella

Tortilla Española/Patata

Tapas

Examples of Mexican Food

Mole Poblano

Tamales

Tostadas

 Nota Cultural

Keep your hands on the table!

Did you know that in many countries it is considered rude to place your hands on your lap during a meal? In the U.S. it is customary to place your hands on your lap during a meal. However, in Europe and Latin America, the custom is different. People keep their hands on the table during a meal.

Ejercicios

Exercise 3.8a:

Directions: Label the place setting.

Exercise 3.8b:

Directions: Write 5 sentences in Spanish to give the placement of the item.

1. La servilleta _____.

2. El plato _____.

3. El cuchillo _____.

4. El platillo _____.

5. La taza _____.

Ejercicios

Exercise 3.8c:

Directions: Tell the use of the item. Follow the example.

Example: Se usan las servilletas para limpiar la cara.

    1. el cuchillo → _____

    2. el tazón → _____

    3. el tenedor → _____

    4. el vaso → _____

    5. la cuchara → _____

Exercise 3.8d:

Directions: Write whether the food is "la comida española" o "la comida mexicana."

    1. Las tapas   _____

    2. Los calamares   _____

    3. Las tostadas   _____

    4. El mole poblano   _____

    5. Las tortillas   _____

Exercise 3.8e:

Directions: Compare Mexican food and Spanish food.

5 Comparisons of Mexican and Spanish Food

    1. _____

    2. _____

    3. _____

    4. _____

    5. _____

SECTION 3.9 - FOOD PYRAMID AND FOOD CHOICES

■ DAY 1

OBJECTIVES

You will learn:

- To demonstrate an understanding of the food pyramid
- To state healthy food choices based on the food pyramid

Food Pyramid

The Food Pyramid provides a guideline to healthy eating. It is published by the US Department of Agriculture to help you choose nutritious food in servings and portions reflective to your activity level.

This section serves to familiarize you with the food pyramid and make you aware of advisable food choices.

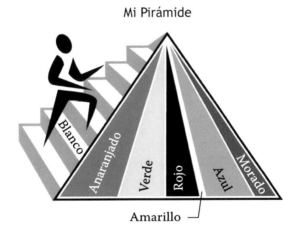

Mi Pirámide

Color de Pirámide	Grupos Alimenticios	Porciones
1. Anaranjado	Los Granos	6 onzas cada día (1oz.= 1 taza de cereal)
2. Verde	Las Verduras	2.5 tazas cada día
3. Rojo	Las Frutas	2 tazas cada día
4. Amarillo	Las Grasas	Limite las grasas
5. Azul	Los Productos Lácteos	3 tazas
6. Morado	Las Carnes y Frijoles	5.5 onzas
7. Blanco	La Actividad Física	30 minutos casi cada día

■ DAY 1

You will learn:

– To state and ask food limits
– To state and ask food consumption

Food Choices

As you know, it is important to make careful food choices that are nutritious and delicious. In doing so, some foods, like vegetables, are better to consume than others. And, you should limit foods high in simple sugar and fat. In this section, you will learn helpful vocabulary to talk about this concept.

Consumir - To Consume

Yo	consumo	= I consume	Nosotros Nosotras	consumimos = we consume
Tú	consumes	= you consume	Vosotros Vosotras	consumís = all of you consume
Él Ella	consume	= he/she consumes	Ellos Ellas	consumen = they consume
Usted (Ud.)	consume	= you (formal) consume	Ustedes (Uds.)	consumen = all of you consume

Limitar - To Limit

Yo	limito	= I limit	Nosotros Nosotras	limitamos = we limit
Tú	limitas	= you limit	Vosotros Vosotras	limitáis = all of you limit
Él Ella	limita	= he/she limits	Ellos Ellas	limitan = they limit
Usted (Ud.)	limita	= you (formal) limit	Ustedes (Uds.)	limitan = all of you limit

Should

In the future you will learn more about the verb "should" or "ought to." However, for the purposes of this section, you will become familiar with the "I" and "you" form of the present tense.

Yo debo   I should

Tú debes   You should

Examples:

¿Debo limitar las grasas?   Should I limit fats?

Sí, debes limitar las grasas.   Yes, you should limit fats.

¿Cuántas verduras debo consumir?   How many vegetable should I consume?

Debes consumir 2.5 onzas cada día.   You should consume 2.5 ounces every day.

 Nota Cultural

Food Pyramid

Did you know that the government produces many of its documents in Spanish and English?
In fact, if you wanted to read all about the Food Pyramid in Spanish, you can. The US Department of Agriculture's website includes an entire section about Mi Pirámide en Español. Log onto: www.mypyramid.gov to check it out.

Ejercicios

Exercise 3.9a:

Directions: In Spanish, write 3 foods or activities that would belong in each category.

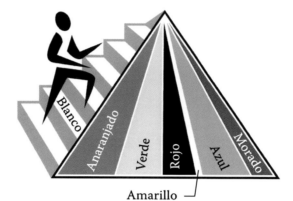

_____

_____

_____

_____

_____

Exercise 3.9b:

Directions: Match the category to the food.

1. _____ el lomo   a. los granos

2. _____ el pan integral   b. las verduras

3. _____ el yogur   c. las frutas

4. _____ el aceite de oliva   d. las grasas

5. _____ la pasta   e. los productos lácteos

6. _____ las ciruelas   f. las carnes y frijoles

7. _____ los frijoles   g. la actividad física

8. _____ la lechuga

9. _____ las berenjenas

10. _____ la mantequilla

Ejercicios

Exercise 3.9c:

Directions: Answer the questions in Spanish.

1. ¿Cuántas porciones de granos debes consumir?
2. ¿Cuántas porciones de frutas debes consumir?
3. ¿Cuántas porciones de carnes y frijoles debes consumir?
4. ¿Cuántas porciones de verduras debes consumir?
5. ¿Cuántas porciones de productos lácteos debes consumir?

Exercise 3.9d:

Directions: Based on what you learned from the Food Pyramid, write 5 sentences advising someone what a person *should limit* and *should consume* in order to eat healthfully.

Tú...   _____

_____

_____

_____

_____

Exercise 3.9e:

Directions: Fill in the correct form the verb.

1. Yo _____ limitar las grasas.

2. Normalmente, no _____ mucho pan.

3. ¿_____ tú las grasas?

4. Mi amiga no _____ la comida buena.

5. Debo _____ 2 tazas de frutas.

SECTION 3.10 - REVIEW OF UNIT 3

■ DAY 1

You will learn:

- To recall the first half of Unit III

Review

At the end of each unit you will review the main concepts in lessons 1-9. In addition, you will use lesson 10 to combine the concepts into one cohesive idea. Because each unit has a theme, the content of each lesson belongs with the other lessons of the unit. Lesson 10 provides the opportunity to combine all concepts to practice your proficiency.

The following outline lists the important concepts from each lesson. Go back to each lesson and review these concepts.

You should be able to explain the concept as well as use the concept in sentences and questions.

Spanish Review Outline

    I. Lesson 1
       A. List Fruits
       B. List Vegetables

    II. Lesson 2
       A. List Proteins
       B. List Vocabulary related to Proteins

    III. Lesson 3
       A. List Carbohydrates
       B. List Desserts

    IV. Lesson 4
       A. List Dairy Products
       B. List Snacks

    V. Lesson 5
       A. List Condiments
       B. List Drinks

■ Day 2

OBJECTIVES

You will learn to:

 – Recall the second half of Unit III

Spanish Review Outline

VI. **Lesson 6**
   A. **Adjectives to Describe Food**
   B. **-ísimo**

VII. **Lesson 7**
   A. **To be Hungry and Thristy**
   B. **Expressions with Food**
   C. **Breakfast, Lunch, and Dinner**

VIII. **Lesson 8**
   A. **Place Settings**
   B. **Spanish Food versus Mexican Food**

IX. **Lesson 9**
   A. **Food Pyramid**
   B. **Food Choices**

Culture Review Outline

In addition to the Spanish concepts, you also learned culture. Please review the culture concepts in this outline.

You should be able to explain each culture concept.

I.   **Lesson 1**
   - **Tropical Fruits**

II. **Lesson 2**
   - **Chorizo**

III. **Lesson 3**
   - **Magdalena Muffins**

IV. **Lesson 4**
   - **Goat's Milk**

V.   **Lesson 5**
   - **Churros con Chocolate**

VI. **Lesson 6**
   - **Chocolate**

VII. **Lesson 7**
   - **Foods of Costa Rica**

VIII. **Lesson 8**
   - **Table Etiquette**

IX. **Lesson 9**
   - **Food Pyramid**

Ejercicios

Exercise 3.10a:

Directions: Categorize these random foods according to type.

La soja	El pudín	El cangrejo	El pastel de carne
El pepino	El atún	El albaricoque	Los frijoles
La harina	La toronja	El pollo	El caramelo
El panecillo	El champiñón	La naranja	La leche
La zanahoria	El jarabe de arce	La cereza	El queso de untar
El arroz	El elote	El helado	La cebolla
La mantequilla	La chuleta	Los espaguetis	Los dulces

Las Frutas   Las Verduras   Los Granos

Las grasas   Los Productos Lácteos   Las Carnes y Frijoles

Exercise 3.10b:

Directions: Answer the questions in Spanish.

1. Identifica 6 bebidas que te gustan:

2. Identifica 6 bebidas que no te gustan:

3. ¿Qué condimento usas cuando comes los perritos calientes?

4. ¿Prefieres: la sal o la pimienta?

5. ¿Es bueno beber el agua?

Ejercicios

Exercise 3.10c:

Directions: Translate the small paragraph.

For dinner, I normally eat baked chicken. I also have a vegetable, like green beans with butter. Sometimes, I make mashed potatoes with butter. They are really tasty. Also, I like to eat dessert like ice cream or chocolate cake with whipped cream. The desserts are really rich and extremely good. My family and I eat dinner together.

_____

_____

_____

_____

_____

_____

Exercise 3.10d:

Directions: Based on the picture, tell the following:

What's being eaten
Description of food
If the person is hungry, thirsty
If it breakfast, lunch, dinner
If the person should (debe) limit or consume other food

_____

_____

_____

_____

_____

Section 3.6 _____ Date

Section 3.7 _____ Date

Section 3.8 _____ Date

Section 3.9 _____ Date
_____
_____
_____
_____
_____
_____
_____
_____

Section 3.10 _____ Date
_____
_____
_____
_____
_____
_____
_____
_____

Additional Notes _____ Date
_____
_____
_____
_____
_____
_____
_____
_____

CLOTHING AND SHOPPING

SECTION 4.1 - BASIC CLOTHING; WHAT ARE YOU WEARING?

■ DAY 1

OBJECTIVES

You will learn:

- To list basic clothing items
- To identify basic clothing items

Basic Clothing

Look at the outfit you're wearing now. Can you name the clothing items in Spanish? Well, if you can't, this section and the subsequent sections will teach you vocabulary in Spanish for clothing.

La Ropa - Clothing

La camisa	Shirt
La camiseta	T-shirt
La camiseta sin mangas	Tank top
El suéter	Sweater
Los pantalones	Pants
Los vaqueros	Jeans
Los tejanos	Jeans
Los jeans	Jeans
Los pantalones cortos	Shorts
La falda	Skirt
El vestido	Dress

Additional Vocabulary

La camisa de vestir	Dress shirt
La camisa de manga larga	Long-sleeved shirt
La camisa de manga corta	Short-sleeved shirt
El suéter con cuello de cisne	Turtleneck sweater
La sudadera	Sweatshirt
Los pantalones de entrenamiento	Sweat pants
La minifalda	Mini-skirt

Event Specific Vocabulary

El traje	Suit
La corbata	Tie
El esmoquin	Tuxedo
El traje de baño	Bathing suit

Examples:

Hay unos vestidos en el armario.	There are dresses in the closet.
Voy a comprar unas camisas.	I am going to buy some shirts.
Me gustan los vaqueros de Rock & Republic®.	I like Rock & Republic® jeans.
No tengo minifaldas.	I don't have mini-skirts.
Para el trabajo, necesito pantalones nuevos y unas camisas de vestir.	For work, I need new pants and some dress shirts.

■ DAY 2

OBJECTIVES

You will learn to:
- To state what people wear/ are dressed in
- To ask what people wear/ are dressed in

What are you wearing?

Before you learn more about clothing items, it is important to know how to say what you and others are wearing. There is more than one way to express this concept in Spanish. The first uses the verb in Spanish "llevar" which means "to wear" or "to carry." The second way uses the verb "vestirse" which has varying meaning on the subject of "dress," or "wear." The conjugations below will assist you in using these verbs in conversation.

Llevar- To Wear, To Carry

Yo	llevo	= I wear/ carry	Nosotros Nosotras	llevamos	= we wear/carry
Tú	llevas	= you wear/carry	Vosotros Vosotras	lleváis	= all of you wear/ carry
Él Ella	lleva	= he/she wears/carries	Ellos Ellas	llevan	= they wear/carry
Usted (Ud.)	lleva	= you (formal) wear carry	Ustedes (Uds.)	llevan	= all of you wear carry

Examples:

Yo llevo unos pantalones y una camisa.   I am wearing pants and a shirt.

Ella nunca lleva las faldas.   She never wears dresses.

Vestirse- To Dress (Oneself), To Get Dressed, To Be Dressed, To Wear

Yo	me visto = I dress (myself)		Nosotros Nosotras	nos vestimos = we dress (ourselves)	
Tú	te vistes = you dress (yourself)		Vosotros Vosotras	os vestís = all of you dress (yourselves)	
Él Ella	se viste = he/she dresses (himself/herself)		Ellos Ellas	se visten = they dress (themselves)	
Usted (Ud.)	se viste = you (formal) dress (yourself)		Ustedes (Uds.)	se visten = all of you dress (yourselves)	

Important Notes about Vestirse

- "Vestirse" translates to mean different things.
- "Vestirse" is a stem-changing verb from e → i.
- The -se at the end is a reflexive pronoun.
- Reflexive means the subject of the verb is doing the action to himself.
    Example: Who is he dressing? He is dressing himself.
- The -se also needs to change into a pronoun that matches the subject/verb.
    Notice how "se" moves from behind the verb to in front of the verb.

Examples

Me visto en una camisa.   I dress (myself) in a shirt.

Se visten en los esmóquines.   They are dressed in tuxedos.

Nota Cultural

Spain Rejects Models Who Are Too Thin

Spain has taken a stand against models that are too thin. In an effort to create a healthy image of beauty for women, Spain decided to monitor the body mass index of models. In 2006, at Spain's top fashion show, the organizers of the pageant used a mathematical formula to calculate a model's body mass index (BMI). The thirty percent of the models that flunked were not chosen to walk the runway. Way to go Spain!

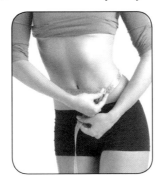

Ejercicios

Exercise 4.1a:

Directions: Match the Spanish to the English.

1. _____ Una camiseta
2. _____ Una camisa de vestir
3. _____ Un vestido
4. _____ Una camisa de manga larga
5. _____ Una camisa de manga corta
6. _____ Una falda
7. _____ Unos tejanos
8. _____ Un traje
9. _____ Un traje de baño

a. a dress
b. a dress shirt
c. a bathing suit
d. a short-sleeved shirt
e. some jeans
f. a suit
g. a skirt
h. a T-shirt
i. a long-sleeved shirt

Ejercicios

Exercise 4.1b:

Directions: *Write sentences to list the clothing items in the closet.*

_____

_____

_____

_____

_____

_____

Exercise 4.1c:

Directions: *According to the paragraph, dress the person by drawing on clothing.*

Esta persona lleva una camiseta sin mangas.
La persona tiene unos pantalones cortos.
También, tiene una sudadera y unos zapatos de tenis.

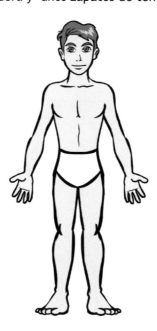

Ejercicios

Exercise 4.1d:

Directions: Fill in the correct form of the verb "llevar."

1. Yo _____ una falda.

2. Nosotros _____ la ropa de Pryca.

3. Ellos _____ los trajes todos los días.

4. ¿Qué vas a _____?

5. Emilio _____ los pantalones cortos en el verano.

Exercise 4.1e:

Directions: Fill in the correct form of the verb "vestirse."

1. Me gusta _____ en la ropa elegante.

2. Yo _____ en los vaqueros.

3. Ellos _____ en camisas de mangas cortas.

4. ¿_____ tú en un esmoquin?

5. Para la escuelas, Uds. no _____ en las minifaldas.

Exercise 4.1f:

Directions: Translate the sentences into English.

1. ¿Qué llevas hoy?
2. Voy a llevar una sudadera y unos pantalones de entrenamiento.
3. ¿A qué hora vas a vestirte?
4. Me visto a las 8:00.
5. Las chicas llevan los suéteres con cuello de cisne y los pantalones.

_____

_____

_____

_____

_____

_____

SECTION 4.2 - OUTERWEAR AND UNDERGARMENTS

■ DAY 1

You will learn to:

-To list outerwear

-To say what outerwear someone is wearing

Outerwear

Outerwear refers to the clothes worn on top of your basic clothing. Outerwear typically changes depending on the weather and type of season. In this section, you will learn the vocabulary in Spanish for outerwear.

Las Prendas Exteriores - Outerwear

La chaqueta	Jacket
La chaqueta vaquera	Jean jacket
La chaqueta de esquiar	Ski jacket
La chaqueta deportiva	Sport jacket
El impermeable	Rain coat
La gabardina	Rain coat
El poncho	Poncho
El sombrero	Hat
La gorra	Cap
La gorra de béisbol	Baseball hat
Los guantes	Gloves
La bufanda	Scarf
Los zapatos	Shoes
Los zapatos de tenis	Sneakers
Las sandalias	Sandals
Los tacones altos	High heels

Examples:

En el invierno, llevo una chaqueta de esquiar.	In the winter, I wear a ski jacket.
Cuando llueve, me visto en un impermeable.	When it rains, I dress in a rain coat.
A veces los tacones altos son incómodos.	Sometimes high heels are uncomfortable.

■ DAY 2

You will learn to:

- To list undergarments
- To state what undergarments there are

Undergarments and Intimate Apparel

Undergarments are clothes worn under your basic clothing. Intimate apparel includes pajamas and other clothing items typically not worn outside the home. In this section, you will learn the vocabulary in Spanish for outer garments and intimate apparel.

La Ropa Interior- Undergarments

La ropa interior	Underwear
La ropa interior larga	Long underwear
La tanga	Thong
Las bragas	Panties
Los calzoncillos	Boxers/briefs
El sujetador	Bra
El sostén	Bra
La camisole	Camisole
Los calcetines	Socks
Las pantimedias	Pantyhose
Las medias panty	Pantyhose
Las medias	Tights
La combinación	Slip
Los pijamas	Pajamas
La bata	Robe/House dress
La lencería	Lingerie

 Nota Cultural

Acceptable Dress

Often, in Spanish-speaking countries, attire is more formal than in the U.S. For example, wearing flip-flops anywhere other than the beach is frowned upon. Furthermore, hats are not worn as part of an outfit, nor are they worn in buildings. This style and custom originated in the U.S. and is not customary elsewhere.

Ejercicios

Exercise 4.2a:

Directions: Draw a picture of the item/s the person is wearing.

1. Juan lleva un sombrero.

2. Magda se viste en pantalones, un poncho y sandalias.

3. Paco lleva una gorra de béisbol.

4. Rafaela se viste en los jeans, un suéter, guantes y una bufanda.

Exercise 4.2b:

Directions: Match the item to the season/s. There may be more than one correct answer.

A. En la primavera o en el otoño.   B. En el invierno.   C. En el verano.

1. _____Las sandalias

2. _____El impermeable

3. _____La chaqueta de esquiar.

4. _____Los guantes

5. _____La bufanda

6. _____La chaqueta vaquera

Exercise 4.2c:

Directions: Write the undergarments or intimate apparel worn for each situation.

1. Una mujer se viste por la mañana.   Va a vestirse en _____.

2. Vas a ir de esquiar.   Vas a llevar _____.

3. Un hombre se viste por la mañana.   Va a vestirse en _____.

4. Ella va a llevar una falda.   Va a llevar _____.

5. Lleva los zapatos.   Necesita llevar _____.

6. Van a dormir (sleep) pronto.   Llevan _____.

Exercise 4.2d:

Directions: Draw the vocabulary word.

1. Los calzoncillos   2. Los pijamas

3. Las medias   4. La ropa interior larga

Exercise 4.2e:

Directions: Match the Spanish to the English.

1. La lencería   a. robe/ house dress

2. El sostén   b. bra

3. Los calcetines   c. slip

4. La combinación   d. lingerie

5. La bata   e. socks

SECTION 4.3 - ACCESSORIES AND COLOR

■ DAY 1

You will learn:

- To list accessories
- To ask and state what accessories a person is wearing

Accessories

Think of the accessories you like to wear. Do you wear a watch? Or, maybe you wear a fashionable bracelet or wristlet that conveys a belief or message. Regardless of the accessory, accessories can compliment any outfit. In this section, you will learn the vocabulary for accessories.

Los Complementos - Accessories

Las joyas	Jewelry
Las bisuterías	Costume jewelry
El reloj	Watch
Digital	Digital
De bolsillo	Pocket
La pulsera	Bracelet
Los aretes	Earrings
Los pendientes	Earrings
De aros	Hoop
Con tachuela/poste	Stud
El anillo	Ring
De diamante	Diamond
Nasal	Nose
El collar	Necklace
El cinturón	Belt
Las gafas	Glasses
Los anteojos	Glasses
Las gafas de sol	Sunglasses
La cinta para el pelo	Headband
La pinza	Barrette/clip
La hebilla	Barrette/clip
La banda elástica	Hair tie
El paraguas	Umbrella
La bolsa	Purse
La cartera	Wallet

Examples

Siempre lleva las gafas de sol cuando hace sol.

      She always wears sunglasses when it's sunny.

Cuando llueve, usa un paraguas y un impermeable.

      When it rains, he uses an umbrella and a rain coat.

Normalmente las mujeres se usan las bolsas.

      Normally women use purses.

No me visto con muchos complementos.

      I don't wear a lot of accessories.

■ DAY 2

OBJECTIVES

You will learn to:
- To list colors
- To identify colors

Color

Because life is filled with color, it is helpful to know the vocabulary for colors in Spanish. After you learn this vocabulary, you will be able to use colors as adjectives in subsequent sections.

Los Colores - Colors

Rojo	Red
Rosado	Pink
Anaranjado	Orange
Amarillo	Yellow
Verde	Green
Azul	Blue
Morado	Purple/violet
Violeta	Purple/violet
Café	Brown
Marrón	Brown
Beige	Beige/tan
Negro	Black
Blanco	White
Gris	Grey
Claro*	Light
Oscuro*	Dark

* Placed after the color

Examples:

¿Qué es tu color favorito?	What is your favorite color?
Mi color favorito es azul claro.	My favorite color is light blue.
¿De qué color es?	What color is it?
Es de color verde oscuro.	It is (of the color) dark green.

 Nota Cultural

State Name: Colorado

Did you know the name for the state of Colorado is Spanish in origin? The name was chosen because of the state's magnificent scenery of mountains, rivers and plains. In fact the state name means "colored red."

Ejercicios

Exercise 4.3a:

Directions: List the vocabulary in the picture in Spanish.

_____

_____

_____

_____

_____

_____

Ejercicios

Exercise 4.3b:

Directions: Answer the questions in Spanish.

1. ¿Prefieres los pendientes de aros o los pendientes con tachuela?
2. ¿Te gustan los anillos nasales?
3. ¿Llevas diarios unos complementos?
4. ¿Qué llevas: una bolsa o una cartera?
5. ¿Normalmente usas un cinturón cuando llevas los pantalones?

Exercise 4.3c:

Directions: Write in Spanish the color of the item/s.

1. A field of grass   _____
2. A pint of strawberries   _____
3. The sun   _____
4. A bunch of violets   _____
5. The sky   _____
6. A candy bar   _____
7. The keys on a piano   _____
8. An orange   _____

Exercise 4.3d:

Directions: Translate into Spanish.

1. It is light pink.   _____
2. My favorite color is dark purple. _____
3. I don't like the color green. _____
4. Do you like yellow?   _____
5. Is orange your favorite color? _____

SECTION 4.4 - COLOR AND FABRIC

■ DAY 1

OBJECTIVES

You will learn:
- To use colors as adjectives

┃ Colors (Continued) ┃

Most of the time, when you use color in conversation, it is to describe something. In this section, you will learn how to use color to describe clothing.

Asking About Color

To ask the color of an item:

¿De qué color es _____?   Of what color is _____?

¿De qué color son _____?   Of what color are _____?

┃ Why must "de" be included? ┃

"De" must be included because the color is a characteristic of the item. For example, if the shirt is blue, the color blue is a characteristic of the shirt. The "de" is used to attach the color, as a descriptive word, to the shirt.

┃ Stating Color ┃

There are a couple of ways to describe items with colors. Some ways to state the color of an item are the following:

La blusa es de color blanco.   The blouse is the color white.

If the color is preceded by the words "de color" in Spanish, then the word for the color does not change. The color becomes part of a phrase describing the noun. However, if the color directly modifies the noun, then it must agree in number and gender with the noun. The examples below show how the color "white" in Spanish is feminine and singular because the noun is feminine and singular.

La blusa es blanca.   The blouse is white.

Es una blusa blanca.   It is a white blouse.

Nouns Used As Adjectives

Sometimes common nouns become color adjectives. Here is a list of some nouns that can become adjectives describing color. Many other nouns can become adjectives describing color. Just think of how many times you do this in English (example: mustard-colored).

Noun	Meaning	Adjective	Meaning
El ámbar	amber	de color de ámbar	amber-colored
El café	coffee	de color de café	coffee-colored
La cereza	cherry	de color de cereza	cherry-colored
El chocolate	chocolate	de color de chocolate	chocolate-colored
La turquesa	turquoise	de color de turquesa	turquoise-colored

Oftentimes, the second "de" is omitted. However, it is included here, as the translation means "of the color of _____." For example, "es de color de chocolate" translates to be "it is the color of chocolate."

■ DAY 2

OBJECTIVES

You will learn to:

- To list fabrics
- To describe clothes by fabrics

Fabrics

An important aspect of clothing is the fabric from which it is made. The fabric can add or detract from the quality and usefulness of the garment. In addition, different fabrics have different effects on clothing. For example a silk shirt would have a very different purpose than a wool shirt. In this section, you will learn the vocabulary for the names of fabrics in Spanish.

Las Telas/Los Tejidos - Fabrics

La fibra natural	Natural fiber
El cuero	Leather
La piel	Fur
El algodón	Cotton
La seda	Silk
La lana	Wool
El lino	Linen
La fibra sintética	Synthetic fiber
El nylon	Nylon
El poliéster	Polyester
El rayón	Rayon
El terciopelo	Velvet
El terciopelo arrugado	Crushed Velvet

Describing Clothing

When you are describing clothing by fabric type, place a "de" after the type of clothing. Then, add the fabric type.

La chaqueta es de cuero.

The jacket is leather.

Voy a vestirme en un vestido de seda.

I am going to put on a silk dress.

En el verano, mi hermano lleva los pantalones de lino.

In the summer, my brother wears linen pants.

 Nota Cultural

South American Leather

Did you know that many countries in South America produce quality leather goods? The reason why many countries, such as Argentina, produce leather goods is because cattle are a good produced by the countries. In fact, in the pampas, or plains, of Argentina, many gauchos, or cowboys, are cattle-ranchers.

Ejercicios

Exercise 4.4a:

Directions: Ask what color the clothing is.

1. The shirt _____

2. The skirt _____

3. The jacket _____

4. The scarf and gloves _____

Ejercicios

Exercise 4.4b:

Directions: Write sentences stating the color of the items.

Umbrella	Yellow
Sneakers	White
Sweatshirt	Red
Suit	Black
Dress	Blue

1. _____

2. _____

3. _____

4. _____

5. _____

Exercise 4.4c:

Directions: Make the noun a color. Follow the example.

Example: Smoke   → el humo   → de color de humo   → smoke- colored.

     Orange   → la naranja   →   →

     Lime   → la lima   →   →

     Grape   → la uva   →   →

     Sand   → la arena   →   →

     Emerald   → la esmeralda   →   →

Exercise 4.4d:

Directions: Circle all of the possible correct answers.

1. Llevarías (you would wear) una camisa de lino...

a. en el verano.   b. en el invierno.   c. en el otoño.   d. en la primavera.

2. Llevarías (you would wear) una chaqueta de lana...

a. en el verano.   b. en el invierno.   c. en el otoño.   d. en la primavera.

3. Llevarías (you would wear) una camisa de terciopelo

a. en el verano.   b. en el invierno.   c. en el otoño.   d. en la primavera.

4. Llevarías (you would wear) los pantalones de poliéster

a. en el verano.   b. en el invierno.   c. en el otoño.   d. en la primavera.

5. Llevarías (you would wear) unos calcetines de algodón

a. en el verano.   b. en el invierno.   c. en el otoño.   d. en la primavera.

Exercise 4.4e:

Directions: Find the vocabulary word in the word search.

Cotton   Leather   Wool   Linen
          Fur   Silk   Velvet

O	J	I	K	H	I	O	Q	W	W	H	O	A	Z	K
A	L	K	V	O	E	U	C	E	I	I	V	U	D	G
K	L	E	R	D	L	H	X	X	A	J	I	N	U	F
K	S	E	P	S	N	N	C	W	N	G	Y	Ó	L	T
D	U	E	A	O	F	Q	I	F	Q	L	P	D	N	W
C	U	T	D	R	I	P	H	M	D	N	R	O	B	F
W	B	V	K	A	G	C	K	K	Z	U	I	G	O	B
G	C	B	O	X	V	L	R	Y	T	D	F	L	Y	S
P	Z	F	J	P	F	A	E	E	Q	M	I	A	L	W
T	U	D	K	V	Z	N	N	L	T	N	Y	Z	T	M
D	S	P	I	E	L	A	V	U	O	X	W	L	Y	Q
B	O	P	W	E	M	J	Y	T	E	B	X	D	R	C
S	G	W	F	L	B	Q	M	G	F	Y	L	T	S	N
P	V	D	N	B	J	X	N	Q	K	U	V	U	R	Y
B	K	Z	R	V	G	K	D	T	Y	D	O	T	J	C

Ejercicios

Exercise 4.4f:

Directions: Ask it in Spanish.

1. Is that shirt rayon?

2. Do you wear fur and leather clothing?

3. Do you like cotton pajamas?

4. Do you wear velvet?

5. Does he prefer natural or synthetic fabric?

_____

_____

_____

_____

_____

SECTION 4.5 - PATTERNS AND DETAILS

■ DAY 1

OBJECTIVES

You will learn:

- To list clothing patterns
- To ask and answer about clothing patterns

Patterns

How many times do you wear a plain article of clothing? Not many, right? Well, as you know, fabrics come in all types of patterns. In this section, you will learn the vocabulary for many different kinds of patterns.

Los Estampados - Patterns

Floral	Floral
A rayas, rayado	Striped
Con rayas multicolores	Candy striped
A lunares	Polka dot
A cuadros	Plaid
Estampado de cachemira	Paisley
Sin estampar	Solid
Liso (placed after the color)	Solid
Estampado animal	Animal print
Teñido anudado	Tied-dyed

Examples:

En las tiendas es difícil encontrar las faldas a cuadros.

In the stores it is hard to find plaid skirts.

Me gusta mucho llevar la ropa a lunares.

I like to wear clothes with polka dots a lot.

Quiero los tacones altos con un estampado animal.

I want high heels with an animal print.

En el trabajo necesitamos llevar las camisas de polo en colores sin estampar.

For work, we need to wear polo shirts in solid colors.

■ DAY 2

You will learn to:

- To incorporate clothing names, colors, fabrics and patterns
- To describe clothing shape

Describir la Ropa

In the last sections, you learned the names of clothing items and accessories as well as how to describe them by color, fabric, and pattern. In this section, you will learn some vocabulary to describe different shirt styles and the different closures for clothing.

Shirt Shape

El cuello	neck
Redondo	round
Cuadrado	square
Vuelto desbocado	cowl
De pico	v-neck
Sin tirantes	strapless
Sin espalda	backless

Closures

La cremallera	a zipper
Los botones	the buttons
La cinta Velcro	the Velcro

Examples:

Para la fiesta voy a vestirme en un vestido sin tirantes.

For the party I am going wear a strapless dress.

Las camisas sin espaldas están de moda.

Backless shirts are in style.

Los pantalones cortos tienen una cremallera.

The shorts have a zipper.

Nota Cultural

Carolina Herrera

Carolina Herrera is one of the most famous designers of the 20th and 21st centuries. And, she is Latin American. Carolina Herrera was born into a wealthy family in Caracas, Venezuela. She learned English at a British school that she attended in Caracas. After a successful career launch in the early 1980s, Carolina moved to the U.S. to begin her career at the age of 40. Carolina's style is chic, sleek, and glamorous. Her style is reflected in her label, as she designs everything in her collection herself. Now, Carolina Herrera produces a fashion collection, a bridal collection, fragrances, color cosmetics and accessories.

Ejercicios

Exercise 4.5a:

Directions: Draw in the pattern.

Estampado a cachemira   Floral   Rayado

Estampado animal   A lunares   A cuadro

Exercise 4.5b:

Directions: Read the sentence. Then, match the pattern to the sentence.

1. _____Ella lleva unos pantalones a cuadro.   A. animal print

2. _____Lleva un vestido a lunares.   B. solid

3. _____La bufanda tiene un estampado animal.   C. floral

4. _____Los guantes verdes lisos son míos.   D. polka dot

5. _____Se viste en una camiseta floral.   E. plaid

Exercise 4.5c:

Directions: Write as many sentences as you can to describe the picture.

_____

_____

_____

_____

Exercise 4.5d:

Directions: Look at what you're wearing. Write five sentences to describe what you're wearing.　Include types of clothing, fabric, print, shirt style, and closures.

_____

_____

_____

_____

_____

Exercise 4.5e:

Directions: Read the paragraph. Then, answer the questions in English to check your comprehension.

Los tops halter, que lleva JLo, están muy de moda esta primavera. Úsalos con unas faldas largas para un look romántico, o con los jeans para un look muy informal o deportivo. También los vestidos tan cortos como posible están muy de moda. Las estrellas enseñan las piernas con los minivestidos y minifaldas. Usan los colores lisos y vivos y las fábricas sin estampados para un look mod.

1. What is in style this spring? _____

2. What is a romantic look? _____

3. Are miniskirts and mini dresses out of style?_____

4. What is the mod look? _____

Exercise 4.5F:

Directions: Translate the sentences.

1. I have a yellow floral cowl neck shirt.

2. I want a blue silk dress shirt with white buttons.

3. She has to buy a red v-neck tank top for school.

4. The mom needs to buy sneakers with Velcro for her son.

5. I like black round neck sweaters more than black square neck sweaters.

Section 4.1 _____ Date

Section 4.2 _____ Date

Section 4.3 _____ Date

Section 4.4 _____ Date

Section 4.5 _____ Date

Additional Notes _____ Date

SECTION 4.6 - CLOTHING FIT

■ DAY 1

You will learn:
- To describe clothing fit

Clothing Fit

As you know, you can describe clothing a couple of ways. One way is to state the characteristics of the clothing, which you learned how to do in the last sections. Another way is to describe clothing by fit. How many times has someone asked you, "Is this shirt too small?" In this section, you will learn how to give an appropriate answer to this question.

Various Fits

Bien	well/good
Mal	bad
Grande	big
Chico	small
Largo	long
Corto	short
Ancho	wide/loose
Flojo	loose
Estrecho	narrow/tight
Apretado	tight
Arrugado	wrinkled
Perfecto	perfect
Muy	very
Demasiado	too (much)
Bastante	enough
Suficiente	enough

How Is It?

To state or ask how the clothing is, use the verb "estar." "Estar" in Spanish translates to mean "is, am, or are." It is used for more temporary situations. Because the fit of the clothing is dependent on the person, it is temporary. For example, a size 0 shirt on a thin woman would be fine, but the same shirt on someone athletic would be too tight. The description of the shirt is temporary and changes with each situation.

Examples:

Los pantalones están muy anchos.

> The pants are very wide/loose.

El traje de baño está bastante bien.

> The bathing suit is good enough.

La chaqueta vaquera está demasiada larga y muy grande.

> The jean jacket is too long and very big.

La falda está apretada y arrugada.

> The skirt is tight and wrinkled.

■ DAY 2

You will learn to:

- To describe how clothes fit people

The Fit of Clothing

In Spanish, the verb "quedar" is used to describe the fit of an article of clothing on people. This verb is typically seen in two forms:

queda — with one item

quedan — with two or more items

When you are referring to whom the clothes fit, you should place the following indirect object pronouns in front of the verb.

Me queda/n- It fits me.

Te queda/n – It fits you.

Le queda/n – It fits him/her.

Nos queda/n – It fits us.

Examples:

Me queda bien.

> It fits me well.

No me queda bien.

> It doesn't fit me well.

Me queda mal.

> It's a bad fit.

¿Cómo te queda?

> How does it fit you?

¿Te queda bien?

> Does it fit you well?

 Nota Cultural

Oscar de la Renta

Oscar de la Renta was born and raised in the Dominican Republic. He left at age 18 to study in Madrid. While living in Spain, he had an apprenticeship with Spain's most renowned clothing designer Cristóbal Balenciaga. Later, Oscar de la Renta came to New York to design the couture collection for Elizabeth Arden. In 1965, he began his own label.

Ejercicios

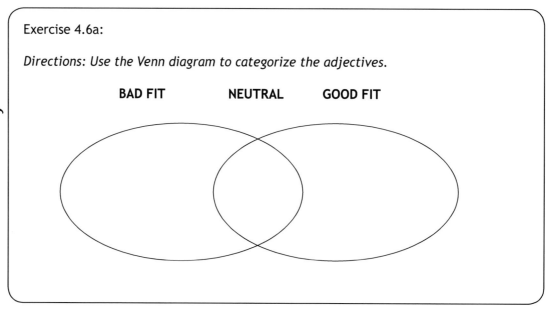

Exercise 4.6a:

Directions: Use the Venn diagram to categorize the adjectives.

BAD FIT   **NEUTRAL**   **GOOD FIT**

Ejercicios

Exercise 4.6b:

Directions: Based on the exclamatory statement, write a sentence to describe the fit of each article of clothing.

1. I LOVE THIS TANK TOP!

_____

2. I CAN'T BUTTON THESE PANTS!

_____

3. I AM SWIMMING IN THIS DRESS!

_____

4. THIS IS THE UGLIEST HAT EVER!

_____

5. I LOOK LIKE I JUST PICKED THIS SUIT OFF OF THE FLOOR!

_____

Exercise 4.6c:

Directions: Go through your closet. Choose 6 clothing items. Write 6 sentences describing how the clothing items fit.

1. _____

2. _____

3. _____

4. _____

5. _____

6. _____

Exercise 4.6d:

Directions: Answer Yes or No according to how you would like the item to fit.

1. La camisa me queda bien. _____

2. Los pantalones me quedan cortos. _____

3. La camiseta me queda grande. _____

4. El suéter me queda apretado. _____

5. La chaqueta me queda perfecta. _____

SECTION 4.7 - SIZING

■ DAY 1

You will learn:
- To size clothing
- To ask and state what size someone wears

Sizing

As you learn Spanish, your desire to travel abroad is probably growing. And, while away, wouldn't you love to go shopping? In this section you will learn clothing sizes so that you will be able to shop for yourself and others.

Las Tallas - Sizes

La talla	The size
El tamaño	The size
Extra Pequeña	XP Extra Small
Pequeña	P Small
Mediana	M Medium
Grande	G Large
Extra Grande	XG Extra Large
Talla Única	One Size Fits All

Stating and Asking Sizes

¿Qué talla usas?

¿Qué talla llevas?

What size do you wear?

Uso el <u>fill in number.</u>

Llevo la talla <u>fill in size.</u>

I wear <u>fill in number or size.</u>

Examples:

La camisa es extra pequeña.	The shirt is extra small.
Uso el 7.5.	I wear a 7.5.
Llevo la talla mediana.	I wear a medium.

■ DAY 2

OBJECTIVES

You will learn:

– To compare international sizing to U.S. sizing

– To ask and state what size someone wears

International Clothing Sizing

Clothing sizes are not international. In fact, there are some basic international size charts. There are sizes for the United Kingdom, for Japan, for the United States, and for Europe. South America and Central America typically use European sizes; however, Mexico and some Central American countries sometimes do not follow this pattern. The comparisons below will show European sizes compared to sizes in the United States. The first chart will compare clothing sizes while the second chart will compare shoe sizes.

Clothing

Men		Women	
U.S.	**European**	**U.S.**	**European**
36	46	6	34
38	48	8	36
40	50	10	38
42	52	12	40
44	54	14	42

Shoes

Men		Women	
U.S.	**European**	**U.S.**	**European**
7	39	4	35
8	41	5	37
9	42	6	38
10	43	7	39
11	45	8	40
12	46	9	42

Examples:

Uso el número 39.

Llevo el número 39.

I wear a 39

 Nota Cultural

Clothing Sizes in Spain

In 2007, in order to promote healthier body image, Spain's government has reached an agreement with major fashion designers to standardize women's clothing. Major Spanish designers such as Cortéfiel, Mango, El Corte Inglés and Inditex, which owns Zara, agreed to take part in the program.

The agreement also states that European size 46 no longer be specifically labeled as a larger size. In addition to standardizing sizes, the Health Ministry will also prevent companies from using windows displays with clothes smaller than a European size 38. Companies will have 5 years to make the change.

Spain's Health Ministry believes that designers should be encouraged to promote a healthy physical realistic to the Spanish population.

Ejercicios

Exercise 4.7a:

Directions: Place the sizes in order from smallest to largest.

_____ talla mediana

_____ talla extra grande

_____ talla extra pequeña

_____ talla pequeña

_____ talla grande

Ejercicios

Exercise 4.7b:

Directions: Answer the questions in a full sentence in Spanish.

¿Qué talla llevas....

De pantalones?   _____

De camisa?   _____

De zapatos?   _____

De chaqueta?   _____

Exercise 4.7c:

Directions: Answer the questions based on the paragraph.

Las tallas de ropa en los Estados Unidos son diferentes a aquellas encontradas en el resto del mundo. Por lo tanto, es importante saber cual es su talla en las medidas de EEUU antes de salir de compras en los Estados. Una guía de ropa puede ayudarle encontrar su talla. Las tallas son aproximadas.

1. True   False   The paragraph is about clothing sizes.
2. True   False   The paragraph states that sizes are different
                        around the world.
3. True   False   The paragraph states that there is a size guide.
4. True   False   The paragraph states that the size comparisons
                        are approximate.

Exercise 4.7d:

Directions: Answer the questions in English to check your comprehension.

1. What European clothing size would you wear?

2. What European shoe size would you wear?

3. Do you agree or disagree with the Health Ministry's agreement
   with fashion designers?

4. Why or why not?

_____

_____

_____

_____

Section 4.8 - Stores; Making a Purchase

■ Day 1

You will learn:
- To identify different types of stores
- To identify the departments of a department store

Stores

You learned in Spanish I, Part 1 an extensive list of stores. In this section, you will learn more names for stores specific to retail and the names of various departments in a department store.

Las Tiendas - Stores

El almacén	Department store
El centro comercial	Mall
El mercado al aire libre	Open air market
La tienda de lujo	Luxury store
La tienda de moda	Clothing store
La tienda de liquidaciones	Discount store

Las Secciones del Almacén

Hogar	Home/housewares
Electrodomésticos	Electrical appliances
Menaje	Kitchenware
Baño	Bath
Habitación	Bedroom
Sofás y Sillones	Sofas and Chairs
Muebles	Furniture
Textil	Textiles
Moda	Fashion/Clothes
Complementos	Accessories
Perfumería	Perfume
Cosmética	Cosmetics
Relojería	Watches
Joyería	Jewelry
Zapatería	Shoes
Electrónica	Electronics
Música	Music
Ocio y Cultura	Leisure
Terraza y Jardín	Patio and Garden
Juguetes	Toys

Examples:

¿Dónde está la sección de terraza y jardín?

> Where is the lawn and garden department?

Está al lado de la sección de electrodomésticos y la joyería.

> It is next to the appliance section and jewelry.

¿Adónde vas para ir de compras?

> Where are you going shopping?

Voy a la tienda de liquidaciones porque hay una promoción de ventas.

> I am going to the discount store (outlet) because there is a sales promotion.

■ DAY 2

OBJECTIVES

You will learn to:

- To list vocabulary related to retail sales and sale items
- To make a purchase in a department store

Making a Purchase

Now that you are able to find a store and the appropriate departments, you probably would like to purchase something. In this section, you will learn the basic vocabulary that will allow you to retail shop.

Comprar Algo - To Buy Something

Ir de compras	To go shopping
Ser una ganga	To be a bargain
Estar a la venta	To be on sale
Hacer una compra impulsiva	To make an impulse buy
Hacer una venta	To make a sale
El mostrador	The counter
La vitrina	The shop window/display case
El registro de ventas	The cash register
La escalera mecánica	The escalator
El vendedor	The sales clerk
El/la cliente/a	The client
La liquidación	The sale
Las rebajas	The sales
La oferta	The bargain
La promoción de ventas	The sale promotion
El precio	The price
El recibo de venta	The sale receipt
El impuesto sobre la venta	The sale tax

Review

Do you remember how to ask/state the cost of an item?

¿Cuánto cuesta/n?

Cuesta/n _____.

Examples:

¿Dónde está el registro de venta?

Where is the cash register?

Está en el mostrador en la sección de cosmética.

It is on the counter in the cosmetic section.

¿Cuánto porcentaje es el impuesto sobre la venta?

What percent is the sales tax?

Es 13%.

It is 13%.

 Nota Cultural

El Corte Inglés

El Corte Inglés is the largest and most popular department store chain in Spain. El Corte Inglés is a symbol of the Spanish culture. The products and services offered by the store cater to the country's diverse regions. Stores tend to be very large in size and offer the finest selection and highest quality goods. There is even a grocery store section to the stores which is located in the basement.

Ejercicios

Exercise 4.8a:

Directions: Unscramble the letters to reveal the store.   Then, solve the hidden phrase.

JODELNIUDETA

DEMDEINAODAT

ASQITOINIDCEDIADUNLEE

RIARAACEEEMDOBILLR

MACLAÉN

LOERAECOCTNRCMI

Exercise 4.8b:

Directions: Answer the questions in complete sentences in Spanish.

1. ¿Dónde compras los juegos?

   _____

2. ¿Adónde vas para comprar una microonda?

   _____

3. ¿En qué sección del almacén te gusta ir de compras?

   _____

4. ¿En qué sección está la ropa?

   _____

5. ¿Qué hay en la relojería?

   _____

Ejercicios

Exercise 4.8c:

Directions: Label as many items as you can in the picture in Spanish.

_____

_____

_____

_____

_____

_____

Exercise 4.8d:

Directions: Complete the conversation by filling in the appropriate vocabulary. Verbs may need to be conjugated.

La clienta:	¿Es Ud. la vendedora de menaje?
La vendedora:	Sí, señora. ¿En qué puedo servirle?
La clienta:	¿Está a la _____ esta sartén en color amarillo?
La vendedora:	Hay una gran _____ de ventas con muchas rebajas. La sartén tiene el precio habitual de 25 euros. Pero, el precio oferta con el descuento al menos de 50 porcentaje ahora está 12.50 _____. Es un precio bajísimo, ¿no?
La clienta:	Sí, mujer. Con los precios tan bajos, es mi oportunidad renovar mis accesorios de cocina.
La vendedora:	En la _____ hay más colores y tamaños diferentes.
La clienta:	Quiero comprar todos tamaños. ¿Cuánto cuesta con el PTA?
La vendedora:	El precio oferta con el impuesto es 17.82 cada uno.
La clienta:	_____ una ganga.
La vendedora:	Pienso que sí también.
La clienta:	Necesito un recibo de _____.
La vendedora:	Claro, no problema.
La clienta:	Gracias.
La vendedora:	Y gracias a Ud.

Ejercicios

Exercise 4.8e:

Directions: Translate the previous conversation.

La clienta: _____

La vendedora: _____

La clienta: _____

La vendedora: _____

La clienta: _____

La vendedora: _____

La clienta: _____

La vendedora: _____

La clienta: _____

La vendedora: _____

La clienta: _____

La vendedora: _____

La clienta: _____

La vendedora: _____

SECTION 4.9 - IN THE DRESSING ROOM

■ DAY 1

You will learn:

- To conjugate more stem changing verbs

More Stem Changing Verbs

Stem changing verbs are verbs that have a change in the stem, or root, when conjugated. As you know from Unit I, there are many stem changing verbs in Spanish.

Stem changing verbs fall into one of three categories. To review the three categories of stem changing verbs:

Before Change		After Change
o	→	ue
e	→	ie
e	→	i

In this lesson, you will see the conjugations for the following four stem changing verbs. Please note that verbs change in the stem, or root, with all subjects except for the "nosotros" and "vosotros" conjugations.

Verb	Meaning	Change
Probar	To try out/on	o → ue
Poder	To be able to, can	o → ue
Perder	To lose	e → ie
Pedir	To ask for	e → i

Probar - To try out/on

Yo pruebo – I try on/am trying on...	Nosotros probamos - We try on /are Nosotras trying on
Tú pruebas - You try on/are trying on	Vosotros probáis - All of you try on / Vosotras are trying on

Él   prueba - He tries on / is trying on
Ella   She tries on /is trying on
Usted (Ud.)   You (formal) try on /are
                                trying on
	Ellos prueban - They try on / are
	Ellas trying on
	Ustedes (Uds.) All of you try on / are
	                                    trying on

Poder -To be able to, can

Yo puedo – I can	Nosotros podemos - We can Nosotras
Tú puedes - You can	Vosotros podéis - All of you can Vosotras
Él puede - He can Ella She can Usted (Ud.) You (formal) can	Ellos pueden - They can Ellas Ustedes (Uds.) All of you can

Perder - To lose

Yo pierdo – I lose	Nosotros perdemos - We lose Nosotras
Tú pierdes - You lose	Vosotros perdéis - All of you lose Vosotras
Él pierde - He loses Ella She loses Usted (Ud.) You (formal) lose	Ellos pierden - They lose Ellas Ustedes (Uds.) All of you lose

Pedir - To ask for

Yo pido - I ask for/ am asking for	Nosotros pedimos - We ask for / are Nosotras asking for
Tú pides - You ask for/ are asking for	Vosotros pedís - All of you ask for/ are Vosotras asking for

Él   pide   - He asks for/ is asking for
Ella   She asks for/ is asking for
Usted (Ud.)   You (formal) ask for/ are
                      asking for
	Ellos piden - They ask for/are asking
	Ellas for
	Ustedes (Uds.) All of you ask for/are
	                            asking for

■ DAY 2

OBJECTIVES

You will learn to:

- ⁻ To try things on in a dressing room in a store
- ⁻ To ask for clothing and sizes
- ⁻ To remark on item tried

In the Dressing Room

It is typical to try on clothing before making a purchase. This section will provide you with the vocabulary needed to converse with sales staff in a dressing room.

En el Vestidor - In the Dressing Room

¿Puedo ayudar en algo?	Can I help you with something?
¿Qué desea?	Can I help you?/ What do you want?
Quiero probármelo.	I want to try (it) on.
Quisiera probármelo.	I would like to try (it) on.
¿Como me lo veo?	How does (it) look on me?
(No) me queda bien.	It does (not). fit me well.
(No) está de moda.	It's (not) in style.
¿Puedes traerme...?	Can you bring me...?
¿Podría traerme...?	Could you bring me...?
otro tamaño	another size
otra talla	another size
otro estilo	another style
algo diferente	something else
Necesito cambiarme de ropa.	I need to change my clothes.

Traer

Traer is a –go verb. If you recall, you already learned about –go verbs. They are verbs that end in –go in the first person present tense. Some other –go verbs you learned are the following: hacer, salir, poner, venir.

Traer – To Bring

Yo	traigo	– I bring	Nosotros Nosotras	traemos	- We bring
Tú	traes	- You bring	Vosotros Vosotras	traéis	- All of you bring
Él Ella Usted (Ud.)	trae	- He brings She brings You (formal) bring	Ellos Ellas Ustedes (Uds.)	traen	- They bring All of you bring

Examples:

¿Puedes traerme otro estilo?   Can you bring me another style?

Tráemelo, por favor.   Bring it to me, please.

Te traigo unas cosas.   I'm bringing you some things.

 Nota Cultural

Sale Shopping in Spain

Are you accustomed to bargain shopping in the U.S.? Well, if you plan to regularly sale in Spain, you may be disappointed. There are only two times a year for store-wide sales. They are in the summer and in January. However, slashed prices are scarce; you will not find discounts great than 50%.

Ejercicios

Exercise 4.9a:

Directions: Write the correct conjugation.

1. They are asking for menus.   _____

2. I am trying on clothes.   _____

3. He loses something every day.   _____

4. We are able to go.   _____

5. I can't buy the shirt.   _____

Exercise 4.9b:

Directions: Correct the errors. Some may be correct.

1. Nosotros pidimos muchas cosas.   _____

2. Ella proba el vestido en el vestidor. _____

3. Vosotros puedéis ayudarme.   _____

4. ¿Puedes venir conmigo?   _____

5. Perde toda la moneda.   _____

Exercise 4.9c:

Directions: Write a statement in Spanish appropriate to the situation.

1. You need another size.   _____

2. You think the item is not in style. _____

3. You want to find out how it looks.   _____

4. Someone is asking to help you.   _____

5. The item does not look good.   _____

Ejercicios

Exercise 4.9d:

Directions: Write a small conversation between you and the sales clerk. Ask him/her to try on something; ask him/her for another size/style/etc.

El vendedor/la vendedora: _____

Yo: _____

El vendedor/la vendedora: _____

Yo: _____

El vendedor/la vendedora: _____

Yo: _____

SECTION 4.10 – REVIEW OF UNIT 4

■ DAY 1

You will learn:

– To recall the first half of Unit IV

Review

At the end of each unit you will review the main concepts in lessons 1-9. In addition, you will use lesson 10 to combine the concepts into one cohesive idea. Because each unit has a theme, the content of each lesson belongs with the other lessons of the unit. Lesson 10 provides the opportunity to combine all concepts to practice your proficiency.

The following outline lists the important concepts from each lesson. Go back to each lesson and review these concepts.

You should be able to explain the concept as well as use the concept in sentences and questions.

Spanish Review Outline

    I. Lesson 1
        A. Basic Clothing
        B. Llevar and Vestirse

"Llevar" means "to wear." You conjugate it as regular -ar verb. You can say what you or someone else is wearing with the verb "llevar."

Example: Llevo una chaqueta.   I am wearing a jacket

"Vestirse" is translated a couple of ways. It means "to dress oneself, to get dressed." It is sometimes also refers to what someone wears.

Example: Me visto en pantalones y una camisa.   I am dressing (myself) in pants and a shirt.

    II. Lesson 2
        A. Outerwear
        B. Undergarments

Use the same verbs in Section 1 to state what outerwear and undergarments that you and others wear.

III. Lesson 3
    A. Accessories
    B. Colors

Use the same verbs in Section 1 to state what accessories you and others wear.

    IV. Lesson 4
      A. Colors as Adjectives
      B. Fabrics

Clothes can be described in many ways.

Examples: Las blusas son azules.   The blouses are blue.

            Los calcetines son de algodón.   The socks are cotton.

V. Lesson 5
    A. Patterns
    B. Describing Clothes

Clothing can also be described by patterns and other details.

Examples:

     Lleva una falda a cuadros.   She wears a plaid skirt.

     La camisa tiene un cuello redondo.   The shirt has a round collar.

■ DAY 2

OBJECTIVES

     You will learn to:
        – Recall the second half of Unit IV

Spanish Review Outline

    VI. Lesson 6
      A. Clothing Fit
      B. Quedar

To say that something fits you well, you say "me queda bien." To say something fits poorly, say "me queda mal."

To be more specific with the fit of clothing, refer to Section 6.

VII. Lesson 7
    A. Sizes
    B. International Clothing Sizes

Las Tallas
Small- Pequeña
Medium- Mediana
Large- Grande

VIII. Lesson 8
    A. Stores
    B. Making a Purchase

There are many different retail stores and departments in department stores in which you can shop.

Review these phrases that will help you to make a purchase.

Ir de compras	To go shopping
Ser una ganga	To be a bargain
Estar a la venta	To be on sale
Hacer una compra impulsiva	To make an impulse buy
Hacer una venta	To make a sale

IX. Lesson 9
    A. Stem Changing Verbs
    B. In the Dressing Room
    C. Traer

Review the stem changing verbs and their changes.

Verb	Meaning	Change
Probar	To try out/on	o → ue
Poder	To be able to, can	o → ue
Perder	To lose	e → ie
Pedir	To ask for	e → i

Remember that traer is a -go verb (yo traigo).

Culture Review Outline

In addition to the Spanish concepts, you also learned culture. Please review the culture concepts in this outline.

You should be able to explain each culture concept.

I. Lesson 1
   - Models in Spain

II. Lesson 2
   - Acceptable Dress

III. Lesson 3
   - Colorado

IV. Lesson 4
   - South American Leather

V. Lesson 5
   - Carolina Herrera

VI. Lesson 6
   - Oscar de la Renta

VII. Lesson 7
   - Clothing Sizes in Spain

VIII. Lesson 8
   - El Corte Inglés

IX. Lesson 9
   - Sale Shopping in Spain

Ejercicios

Exercises 4.10a:

Directions: Practice describing the articles of clothing.

1.   White purse

2.   Striped pants

3.   Wool jacket

4.   Cotton pajamas

5.   Red-polka dotted bathing suit

_____

_____

_____

_____

_____

Exercise 4.10b:

Directions: Write a description of the outfits.

_____

_____

_____

_____

_____

Ejercicios

Exercise 4.10c:

Directions: Write out the Spanish for the following situation.

Situation
You are going shopping.
You wear a size small shirt.
You like a shirt and it fits you well.

_____

_____

_____

Exercise 4.10d:

Directions: Match the meaning.

1. _____ ¿Como me lo veo?	A. Can I help you?
2. _____ ¿Te queda bien?	B. I am going shopping.
3. _____ ¿Qué talla usas?	C. What size do you wear?
4. _____ Está de moda.	D. It's in style.
5. _____ Voy de compras.	E. How does it look on me?
6. _____ ¿Cuánto cuesta/n?	F. Does it look good on you?
7. _____ ¿Puedo ayudar en algo?	G. How much does it cost?

Section 4.6 _____ Date

Section 4.7 _____ Date

Section 4.8 _____ Date

Section 4.9 _____ Date

Section 4.10 _____ Date

Additional Notes _____ Date

ANSWER KEY

Section 1.1

Ejercicio 1.1a:

1. Falso
2. Falso
3. Cierto
4. Cierto
5. Cierto
6. Cierto
7. Cierto
8. Cierto
9. Falso
10. Falso

Ejercicio 1.1b.

1. ¿Dónde está la ropa?
2. ¿Dónde está la mesa?
3. ¿Dónde está la alfombra?
4. ¿Dónde está la lámpara?
5. ¿Dónde está la ventana?

Ejercicio 1.1c.

in this picture you will need to the bed on top of the rug the lamp to the left the window to the right the door next to window and the chair in front of the window

Ejercicio 1.1d.

1. Yo _ESTOY__ allí.
2. Nosotros __ESTAMOS___ lejos de California.
3. Miguel __ESTá___ encima de la silla.
4. Los estéreos __ ESTá N____ en mi casa.
5. Uds. __ ESTá N_____ aquí.
6. ¿Dónde __ ESTás___ tú?

Ejercicio 1.1e.

1. The picture of them near the table goes with number 1.
2. The picture of them far from the table goes with number 2.
3. The picture of them under the table goes with number 3.
4. The picture of them on top of the table goes with number 4.
5. The picture of them next to the table goes with number 5.

Ejercicio 1.1f.

1. No estoy aquí.
2. No estás allí.
3. Estamos en Costa Rica.
4. Las sillas están al lado de la mesa.
5. El reloj está al lado de la ventana.
6. ¿Dónde estáis? Or ... ¿Dónde están?

Section 1.2

Ejercicio 1.2a.
1. El restaurante
2. El centro comercial
3. El correo
4. El cine
5. La biblioteca
6. El supermercado
7. El gimnasio
8. La piscina
9. El hospital
10. La casa

Ejercicio 1.2b.
1. Iglesia
2. Templo
3. Mezquita
4. Sinagoga

Ejercicio 1.2c.
1. You should have drawn Miguel at the supermarket.
2. You should have drawn Miguel at the bank.
3. You should have drawn Miguel at the mall.
4. You should have drawn Miguel at church.
5. You should have drawn Miguel at the post office.

Ejercicio 1.2d.
1. NONE
2. DE LA
3. NONE
4. DEL
5. NONE
6. DE LA
7. DE LA
8. DEL

Ejercicio 1.2e.
El museo está a la izquierda de la plaza.
La tienda está a la derecha de la plaza.
La piscina está en la plaza.
El gimnasio está delante (enfrente) de la plaza.
La escuela está detrás de la plaza.

Ejercicio 1.2f.
1. ¿Está la tienda cerca de la biblioteca?
2. ¿Está el gimnasio lejos de la casa?
3. ¿Está la mezquita al lado del restaurante?
4. ¿Están los cines detrás del centro comercial?
5. ¿Están mis amigos delante (enfrente) de la escuela?

Section 1.3

Ejercicio 1.3a.
1. Praying
2. saving/putting money in the bank
3. borrowing a book
4. doing exercises
5. going shopping
6. spending time with friends
7. surfing the web
8. mailing something
9. walking through a museum looking at the exhibits
10. staying in a hotel

Ejercicio 1.3b.
1. c. or d.
2. o.
3. i.
4. n.
5. g.
6. h.
7. a.
8. m.
9. l.
10. k.
11. c. or d.
12. e.
13. f.
14. b.
15. j.

Ejercicio 1.3c.
1. Yo presto libros. Navego en la red. Bajo información.
2. Elena trabaja.
3. Nosotros comemos y bebemos.
4. Ellos rezan.
5. Mi madre camina con el perro.
6. Tú tienes un examen médico.
7. Mi padre envía por correo.
8. Uds. ven una exposición.
9. Vosotros hacen noche.
10. Yo nado.

Ejercicio 1.3d.
1. Cuando estamos en el parque caminamos con el perro.
2. Cuando están en el correo envían por correo.
3. Cuando estoy en la biblioteca presto muchos libros.
4. Cuando Rebela está en el centro comercial le gusta ir de compras.
5. Cuando estoy en una mezquita me gusta rezar.

Ejercicio 1.3e.
1. ¿Cuándo trabajas?
2. ¿Cuándo pasas tiempo con amigos?
3. ¿Cuándo estudias?
4. ¿Cuándo haces ejercicios?

Ejercicio 1.3f.
1. Falso
2. Cierto
3. Falso
4. Cierto
5. Cierto

Section 1.4

Ejercicio 1.4a.

1. __VOSOTROS___ no vais al hospital porque no tenéis tiempo.
2. _____YO_____ voy a la tienda para ir de compras.
3. _____ELLOS_____ van al concierto esta noche.
4. ____NOSOTROS_____ vamos a la fiesta con nuestros amigos.
5. ___ELLA_____ va a la casa de su novio (boy friend).
6. _____Tú_____ no vas hoy porque estás enfermo.
7. ¡____YO_____ no voy!
8. ____ÉL_____ va al supermercado con su madre.

Ejercicio 1.4b.
1. Tú y yo vamos a la tienda.
2. Migueleña y Graciela van a la sinagoga.
3. José va al trabajo.
4. Tú vas a la biblioteca.
5. Yo voy al banco.

Ejercicio 1.4c.
1. Ana va _____AL_____ correo para comprar sellos.
2. Ana está cerca ____DEL_____ correo.
3. Ana está en ___NOTHING_____ el correo.
4. Beto está en __NOTHING_____ la piscina.
5. Beto va ___A LA_____ piscina.
6. Beto está detrás ___DE LA_____ piscina.

Ejercicio 1.4d.
1. Bernardo _____¿Adónde va (Bernardo)?_____
2. Mónica y tú _____¿Adónde va (Mónica y tú)?_____
3. Ellos _____¿Adónde van (ellos)? _____
4. Tú _____¿Adónde vas (tú)? _____
5. Uds. _____¿Adónde van (Uds.)? _____

Ejercicio 1.4e.
Elide va al banco.
Manolo va a la escuela.
Xav y tú van/vais al parque.
Emilio y Eric van al gimnasio.
Tú vas al hotel.

Ejercicio 1.4f.
Answers will vary but should follow this format with these subjects and verbs.
1. Mi familia y yo vamos al restaurante.
2. Yo voy al gimnasio, a la piscina, o al parque.
3. Yo voy a casa.
4. Mis amigos van al centro comercial, al cine, o a la plaza.

Section 1.5

Ejercicio 1.5a.
1. __d.__El dulce
2. __e.__La gasolina
3. __c. __El pescado
4. _a. ___La verdura
5. _b. ___El pastel

Ejercicio 1.5b.
1. Yo voy a la florería.
2. Yo voy a la panadería.
3. Yo voy a la frutería.
4. Yo voy a la librería.
5. Yo voy a joyería.

Ejercicio 1.5c.
Papelería
Zapatería
Carnicería
Heladería
Juguetería

Ejercicio 1.5d.
1. Voy a la juguetería para comprar unos juegos.
2. Voy a la carnicería para comprar las carnes.
3. Voy a la panadería para comprar el pan.
4. Voy a la papelería para comprar papel y hacer fotocopias.
5. Voy a la heladería para comprar y tomar helado.

Ejercicio 1.5e.
1. En una frutería, se venden ____las frutas_____.
2. En una pescadería, se venden __los pescados_____.
3. En una dulcería, se venden ___los dulces_____.
4. En una gasolinera, se venden ___las gasolinas_____.
5. En una pastelería, se venden __los pasteles_____.
6. En una florería, se venden ___las flores_____.
7. En una librería, se venden __los libros_____.
8. En una juguetería, se venden __los juguetes/los juegos_____.

Ejercicio 1.5f.
Answer will vary- Check example for correctness of activity.

Section 1.6

Ejercicio 1.6a.
1. <u>Voy</u> a ir de compras en el mercado esta tarde.
   I am going to go shopping in the market this afternoon.
2. Las señoras <u>van</u> a hacer ejercicio en el gimnasio esta noche después de trabajar.
   The women are going to exercise in the gym tonight after work.
3. <u>Voy</u> a ir a tomar helado con mi primo a la heladería que está al lado del parque.
   I am going to go to eat ice cream with my cousin in the ice cream shop that's next to the park.
4. ¿<u>Vamos</u> a caminar con nuestro perro nuestro mañana por la mañana?
   Are we going to walk our dog tomorrow in the morning?
5. Ricardo <u>va</u> a bajar información en la biblioteca.
   Ricardo is going to download information at the library.

Ejercicio 1.6b.

Answers may vary but should follow the format.

1. Primero, _yo voy a levantar peso en el gimnasio._____
2. Después, _yo voy a estudiar y aprender en la escuela._____
3. Luego, __yo voy a comer y bebe en el Pollo Frito Kentucky._____
4. Al mediodía, __yo voy a descansar en la plaza._____
5. Después, __yo voy estudiar más en la escuela._____
6. Por fin, __yo voy a mirar la televisión en casa.___

Ejercicio 1.6c.

1. F
2. T
3. F
4. T
5. F

Ejercicio 1.6d.

1. Falso
2. Falso
3. Cierto
4. Cierto

Ejercicio 1.6e.

1. Ronaldo va a las lecciones de piano los lunes.
2. Los domingos, Ronaldo va al templo.
3. Los sábados, Ronaldo va a los conciertos.
4. Normalmente Ronaldo no hace nada los viernes.
5. El viernes, el 3, Ronaldo tiene un examen médico.

Ejercicio 1.6f.

1. No
2. Sí
3. Sí
4. Sí
5. No
6. Sí

Section 1.7

Ejercicio 1.7a.

1. Yo ___VENGO_____ a la fiesta.
2. Quieres ___VENIR_____ al baile, ¿no?
3. Verónica y Melina ___VIENEN_____ a la biblioteca para estudiar a las 6.
4. Vosotros _____VENÍS_____ cuando tenéis tiempo.
5. ¿__VIENES_____ tú con mi hermana?
6. Leonardo no ___VIENE_____ porque tiene que trabajar.

Ejercicio 1.7b.

Answers may vary but here is an example of appropriate answers.

1. ¿Quieres venir al centro comercial?
2. ¿Vas a venir a cenar?
3. Te invito a ir al cine.
4. ¿Vienes conmigo?

Ejercicio 1.7c.
Answers may vary, but here is a sample of correct possible answers.
1. Sí, quiero ir contigo.
2. Fantástico/a. ¿Cuándo y adónde?
3. Sí, vamos ahora.
4. Sí, voy contigo.

Ejercicio 1.7d.
1. Miguel va a la escuela. Mike goes to school. Miguel is not at the school. Miguel is moving farther away from the speaker.
2. Miguel viene a la escuela. Mike comes to school. Miguel is not at the school, but the person who is speaking is at the school. Miguel is moving closer to the speaker.

Ejercicio 1.7e.
1. <u>Toward</u>   Away   Juan y yo venimos a visitar.
2. <u>Toward</u>   Away   Miranda viene pronto.
3. <u>Toward</u>   Away   Quieren venir conmigo.
4. Toward   <u>Away</u>   Quieren ir a la heladería.
5. <u>Toward</u>   Away   Tú vienes a la fiesta.

Ejercicio 1.7f.
To:
From:
Subject:

Querido/a _____,

Answers will vary but the letter must include "te invito."

Hasta pronto, _____

Section 1.8

Ejercicio 1.8a.
Summary: There are two people who see each other in passing. The one girl asks the other girl where she's going. The other girl states that she is going to the library to study. This happens to be where the first girl is going. So, she asks the other girl to go with her. The other girl asks when she's going, which happens to be in 5 minutes. So, the girl agrees to join her.

Ejercicio 1.8b.
1. Ellos ___SALEN_____ del gimnasio muy pronto.
2. Yo ___SALGO_____ con mi novio.
3. Nosotros __SALIMOS_____ de nuestra casa en una hora.
4. Juanita __SALE_____ con Jorge.
5. Uds. __SALEN_____ del museo cuando se cierra.

Ejercicio 1.8c.
Answers will vary- and I will not be able to give an example until I have the comic strip.

Ejercicio 1.8d.
1. La ropa ___CUESTA_____ mucho dinero.
2. Yo __VUELVO_____ de Europa en abril.
3. En 2 idiomas, el español y el ingles, tú __CUENTAS_____ con los números de 0 a 199.
4. Ellos ___VUELVEN_____ de las vacaciones en un día.
5. Cuando duermo, nunca _SUEñO_____.

Ejercicio 1.8e.
1. Mi padre regresa/vuelve de la tienda.
2. Mi madre regresa/vuelve del supermercado
3. Mi hermano regresa/vuelve de la escuela.
4. Mi hermana regresa/vuelve de la piscina.

Ejercicio 1.8f.
1. _j__, _k__ He returns
2. _b__, _h__ They return
3. _d__, _i__ All of you return
4. _f__, _g__ You return
5. __a_, _c__ I return
6. _e__, _l__ We return

Section 1.9

Ejercicio 1.9a.

```
U V G X Q L L M X W K Y S A K
K K D X W K E T T X P X C T M
L O S I E N T O E L Y Y S I D
Z I Z U V O I R V A X E M C A
S J P U C M Y P M K N I F A F
B V O U G X K O N A V V W N N
U T B Y E E Q M L C K V V U N
C H C X S D M P S R N V K O R
A Í D O R T O Z E V L A T G O
T A A D K G C I Z A X I G N M
T K R V N I A R R B Z L Q E V
Z U W E R A A H M W Z B C T V
V V T L P J S M L C B Z X H Z
W H E Q M Z O G Q X T T B F P
N D Y R L W M D C B S H I V T
```

Ejercicio 1.9b.
Across
5. Me gustaría ir.
Down
1. ¿Te gustaría ir?
2. Claro que sí.
3. No sé.
4. Ya me voy.

Ejercicio 1.9c.
1. Cierto
2. Cierto
3. Cierto
4. Falso

Ejercicio 1.9d.
    c
    b
    g
    d
    i
    f
    e
    a
    h

Ejercicio 1.9e.
1. Estoy ocupado/a.
2. Estoy triste.
3. Estoy enfermo/a.
4. Estoy contento/a.
5. Estoy cansado/a.

Section 1.10

Ejercicio 1.10a.
Answers will vary.

Ejercicio 1.10b.
Answers will vary.

Ejercicio 1.10c.
THIS IS ONE IDEA OF A CONVERSATION- ANSWERS WILL VARY.
Fernando: Hola.
Julieta: Hola.
Fernando: Te invito a estudiar conmigo. ---INVITATION
Julieta: ¿Adónde vamos a estudiar?
Fernando: Vamos a ir a la biblioteca. --- PLACE, GOING TO GO
Julieta: : ¿Dónde está la biblioteca?---LOCATION OF PLACE
Fernando: Está cerca de tu casa.---LOCATION OF PLACE
Julieta: Tal vez me voy. ¿Cuándo vamos a salir y regresar? – LEAVE AND RETURN
        - VOCAB FOR MAKING PLANS
Fernando: Salimos ahora y vamos a regresar esta tarde.- LEAVE AND RETURN
Julieta: Bueno. ¡Vamos!--- LET'S GO!

Section 2.1

Ejercicio 2.1a.
1. la clase de arte
2. la clase de ciencias sociales
3. la clase de ciencias
4. la clase de matemáticas
5. la clase de educación física
6. la clase de inglés

Ejercicio 2.1b.
1. Falso
2. Cierto
3. Falso
4. Cierto
5. Cierto

Ejercicio 2.1c.
1. g.
2. a.
3. j.
4. e.
5. i.
6. h.
7. d.
8. b.
9. c.
10. f.

Ejercicio 2.1d.
1. b.
2. c.
3. a
4. c.
5. d.

Ejercicio 2.1e.
1. Arturo has 5 classes.
2. He eats lunch at noon/ 12:00.
3. His career will probably deal with math, science, and computers.

Ejercicio 2.1f.
1. ¿Estudias el alemán?
2. ¿Qué es tu horario?
3. ¿Tienes muchas clases?
4. ¿Cuántas clases de ciencias tienes?
5. Éste es mi horario.

Section 2.2

Ejercicio 2.2a.
1. interesante
2. fácil
3. divertido
4. aburrido
5. difícil

Ejercicio 2.2b.
1. Ilógica
2. Lógica
3. Lógica
4. Lógica
5. Lógica

Ejercicio 2.2c.
Answers may vary but here are some possibilities.
1. La geometría es fácil.
2. El coro y el arte son divertidos.
3. La química es a las 3:00.
4. Sí, el francés es interesante.

Ejercicio 2.2d.
1. Acabo de tener clase.
2. Acabamos de estudiar para el examen.
3. Mis amigos acaban de ir al centro comercial.
4. Mi madre acaba de caminar con el perro.
5. Uds. Acaban de hacer la tarea. / Vosotros acabáis de hacer la tarea.

Ejercicio 2.2e.
1. b, c, d, a
2. c, d, e, a, b

Ejercicio 2.2f.
1. c.
2. d.
3. a.
4. e.
5. b.

Section 2.3

Ejercicio 2.3a.
Reorder: f., b, i, e, a, j, g, d, h, c

Ejercicio 2.3b.
En la primera hora, Vivian tiene el inglés. En la segunda hora, Vivian tiene el español. En la tercera hora, Vivian tiene la biología. En la cuarta hora, Vivian tiene el coro. En la quinta hora, Vivian tiene el almuerzo. En la sexta hora, Vivian tiene la educación doméstica. En la séptima hora, Vivian tiene las matemáticas. En la octava hora, Vivian tiene el salón de estudios. En la novena hora, Vivian tiene la informática. En la décima hora, Vivian tiene el arte.

Ejercicio 2.3c.
Mistakes are underlined.
1. Es el primer<u>o</u> día de clases. - remove the "-o" from "primer"
2. En la cuart<u>o</u> hora, tiene el coro. - change the "-o" to an "-a"
3. Es la 8<u>th</u> clase. - change the "8th" to "8ª"
4. Tiene el español en la 2<u>nd</u> hora. - change "2nd" to "2ª"

Ejercicio 2.3d.
__3__ Luego, tengo el almuerzo.
__5__ Por fin, tengo el salón de estudios.
__1__ Primero, tengo la clase de francés.
__4__ Después del almuerzo, tengo el inglés.
__2__ Próximo, tengo las matemáticas.

Ejercicio 2.3e.
1. Tengo mucha tarea; __no obstante_____, no me molesta porque voy a pasar tiempo con mis amigos esta tarde.
2. Ella tiene dos hermanos; __ también_____, yo tengo dos hermanos.
3. Me gusta mucho ayudar a mi madre en casa. __Por ejemplo_____, yo saco la basura y lavo la ropa.
4. Tengo que estudiar __antes____ de tomar el examen mañana.
5. Tengo el arte a las 11:00. ___Después___, tengo el alemán a las 12:00.

Ejercicio 2.3f.
1. Despúes de la lectura, tengo las ciencias.
2. Luego (Entonces), tengo el español.
3. Me gusta el arte; no obstante, no tengo la clase de arte.
4. Él es muy inteligente; por ejemplo, estudia la física.
5. Antes de ir, quiero comer.

Section 2.4

Ejercicio 2.4a.
1. b
2. d
3. g
4. c
5. f
6. e
7. a

Ejercicio 2.4b.
1. Sí, Pilar y Ernesto van a la misma escuela.
2. Los profesores de Pilar son la Sra. Ramos Ortega y el Sr. Gonzáles.
3. Ellos tienen la educación física en la quinta hora.
4. La Sra. Ramos Ortega es estricta.
5. Ernesto va a la clase de español.

Ejercicio 2.4c.
1. La Sra. Adams es la subdirectora.
2. El Sr. Allegro es el entrenador de tenis.
3. La Srta. Amante es la trabajadora social.
4. El Dr. Apache es el consejero/asesor académico.
5. La Sra. Arnez es la conductora autobús.

Ejercicio 2.4d.
1. La clase de matemáticas es mi favorita.
2. El arte es mi clase favorita.
3. El Sr. López es mi profesor favorito.
4. Son mis favoritos.
5. No es mi favorito.

Ejercicio 2.4e.
Comparison: Both scales are parallel.

Section 2.5

Ejercicio 2.5a.
1. La calculadora
2. La goma de borrar
3. El diccionario
4. El lápiz, el bolígrafo, el papel
5. El libro
6. La regla
7. El sacapuntas

Ejercicio 2.5b.
1. Hay 5 (cinco) plumas/bolígrafos.
2. Hay 2 (dos) impresoras.
3. Hay 3 (tres) mochilas.
4. Hay 1 (una) computadora.
5. Hay 8 (ocho) lápices.

Ejercicio 2.5c.
1. c
2. h
3. i
4. f
5. e
6. d
7. b

Ejercicio 2.5d.
In the pictures of the social studies class, there are 20 student disks and chairs. Mrs. Alvarez's desk is in front of the student desks. To the left, there is a book shelf and a bulletin board. To the right, there is a coat rack and a U.S. flag. Behind the student desks, there is a chalk board. On the ceiling, there are two lights. There aren't any windows. There is a door to the right of the chalkboard.

Ejercicio 2.5e.
1. el pechero
2. la bandera
3. el suelo
4. el estante
5. el tablón de anuncios
6. la pared
7. la pizarra
Secret Phrase: Spanish is fun!

Ejercicio 2.5f.
1. El aula tiene un techo, un suelo, y cuatro paredes.
2. Hay un estante y un pechero.
3. Escribo en la pizarra.
4. Necesito poner la ropa en el armario.
5. Tenemos una bandera de México.

Section 2.6

Ejercicio 2.6a.
1. Me _faltan___ los cuadernos.
2. Me _falta____ el libro de español.
3. Me _falta_____ mucho papel.
4. Me _faltan____ mis papeles.
5. Me _falta____ una calculadora para la clase de matemáticas.

Ejercicio 2.6b.
1. Me faltan un lápiz y una goma de borrar.
2. Me falta la mochila.
3. Me falta la tarea.
4. Me faltan las reglas.
5. Me falta un cuaderno.

Ejercicio 2.6c.
1. Rodolfo va porque le faltan muchas cosas.
2. Le faltan cosas escolares: una mochila, un diccionario, y una calculadora.
3. Sí, Rodolfo invita a Margarita.

Ejercicio 2.6d.
1. C
2. E
3. D
4. A
5. B

Ejercicio 2.6e.
1. Me falta el sacapuntas.
2. A Julio le faltan los lápices.
3. Nos faltan la regla, el lápiz, y la goma de borrar.
4. Les falta la carpeta.
5. Nos faltan los cuadernos.

Ejercicio 2.6f.
1. "El ropero" is to "el armario" as __el asiento____ is to "la silla."
2. "El póster" is to "el cartel" as __el afiche__ is to "el cartel."
3. "Notebook" is to "el cuaderno" as __el cuaderno____ is to "el agenda."
4. "La cosa" is to __el objeto____ as "el aparador" is to "el armario."
5. "El ordenador" is to __la computadora___ as "la pluma" is to "el bolígrafo."

Section 2.7

Ejercicio 2.7a.
El gimnasio
El vestuario
El comedor
La biblioteca
La enfermería
El vestíbulo
El laboratorio (de investigación)
Los salones de clases
Los casilleros (escolares)
El auditorio

Ejercicio 2.7b.
1. Se usa
2. Se usan
3. Se usa
4. Se usan
5. Se usa

Ejercicio 2.7c.
Answers may vary, but here are some possibilities.
1. El gimnasio está lejos de las aulas.
2. El aula 101 está detrás del laboratorio.
3. Los casilleros están al lado de las aulas.
4. El vestuario está cerca del gimnasio.
5. El laboratorio está entre de las aulas.

Ejercicio 2.7d.

			Past Participle	Meaning
1.	Cambiar	→	___Cambiado_____	_____Changed_____
2.	Aburrir	→	___Aburrido_____	_____Bored_____
3.	Situar	→	___Situado_____	_Situated/Located_
4.	Perder	→	___Perdido_____	____Lost_____
5.	Organizar	→	___Organizado____	__Organized_____
6.	Compartir	→	___Compartido____	__Shared_____
7.	Beber	→	___Bebido_____	__Drunk_____
8.	Divorciar	→	___Divorciado_____	__Divorced_____
9.	Frustrar	→	___Frustrado_____	__Frustrated_____
10.	Divertir	→	___Divertido_____	__Fun/Amusing___

Ejercicio 2.7e.
1. La puerta está cerrada.
2. El perro está perdido.
3. Los salones de clases están situados/ubicados cerca de mi casillero.
4. La ropa está lavada y limpiada.
5. La enfermería está situada/ubicada al lado del auditorio.

Ejercicio 2.7f.

	Answer	Correction
1.	Incorrect	Words that ends in –ado or –ido are past participles in the Spanish language.
2.	Incorrect	To form the past participle of an –ar verb, drop the –ar, then add –ado.
3.	Correct	
4.	Incorrect	A past participle can NEVER be used in place of conjugated verbs.
5.	Correct	
6.	Correct	
7.	Correct	

Section 2.8

Ejercicio 2.8a.
Este mes, he viajado a México. He estado dos semanas en Cuernavaca. Mis amigos y yo nos hemos divertido mucho. Mis amigos y yo hemos visto muchos lugares preciosos. Hemos usado mucho la lengua de español durante mi visita. Voy a regresar a los lugares que he estado. Mis amigos, que me acompañaron, ya han regresado. He pensado en salir mañana, pero me faltan muchas cosas importantes tales como mi pasaporte y mi boleto de avión. Mi madre ha pagado por mi boleto de avión pero todavía no lo tengo. Tan pronto como tenerlo, me voy.

Ejercicio 2.8b.
1. Ellos ___HAN_____ compartido muchas cosas.
2. Ella ____HA_____ leído los libros.
3. Yo ___HE_____ encontrado el dinero.
4. ¿___HAS_____ tú perdido algo?
5. Nosotros __HEMOS_____ lavado la ropa esta semana.
6. ¿__HABÉIS_____ estado a Argentina, vosotros?
7. La vista (the view) __HA_____ cambiado, ¿no?

Ejercicio 2.8c.

1. They have shared many things.
2. She has read the books.
3. I have found the money.
4. Have you lost something?
5. We have washed the clothes this week.
6. Have all of you been to Argentina?
7. The view has changed, hasn't it?

Ejercicio 2.8d.

Yo	HE LLEGADO.	I have arrived.	Nosotros	HEMOS LLEGADO.	We have arrived.
Tú	HAS LLEGADO.	You have arrived.	Vosotros	HABÉIS LLEGADO.	All of you have arrived.
Él, Ella, Usted	HA LLEGADO.	He/she has arrived. You have arrived.	Ellos, Ustedes	HAN LLEGADO.	They have arrived. All of you have arrived.

Yo	HE VESTIDO.	I have dressed.	Nosotros	HEMOS VESTIDO.	We have dressed.
Tú	HAS VESTIDO.	You have dressed.	Vosotros	HABÉIS VESTIDO.	All of you have dressed.
Él, Ella, Usted	HA VESTIDO.	He/she has dressed. You have dressed.	Ellos, Ustedes	HAN VESTIDO.	They have dressed. All of you have dressed.

Ejercicio 2.8e.
1. No hemos tenido el tiempo.
2. Has sido un buen amigo.
3. He estado a Costa Rica.
4. Ha trabajado esta semana.
5. Me han confundido.

Ejercicio 2.8f.
1. Tener
2. Haber
3. Tener
4. Haber
5. Tener

Section 2.9

Ejercicio 2.9a.
1. f.
2. g
3. b
4. c
5. d
6. e
7. a

Ejercicio 2.9b.
1. muerto
2. visto
3. hecho
4. escrito
5. impreso

Ejercicio 2.9c.
1. Juanita ha frito la comida.
2. Julieta ha abierto la puerta.
3. Xavier y Rosana han resuelto el problema.
4. Rogelio ha ido a Bolivia.
5. Mateo y Cataldo han hecho la pizza.

Ejercicio 2.9d.
1. Construir
2. Reducir
3. Haber
4. Cubrir
5. Destruir
6. They are not formed from the same root words.

Ejercicio 2.9e.
1. b. Hecho
2. a. Resuelto
3. b. Tenido
4. b. Vuelto
5. a. Descubierto
6. b. Escrito
7. a. Reabierto
8. a. Ido
9. a. Introducido
10. b. Reconstruido
11. b. Muerto
12. a. Puesto
13. a. Roto
14. b. Visto
15. a. Obstruido

Ejercicio 2.9f.
1. He traducido el español.
2. La chica ha obtenido el libro.
3. Hemos conducido el coche (el carro).
4. Ya han subscrito.
5. ¿Has reabierto la ventana?

Section 2.10

Ejercicio 2.10a.
Answer may vary, but can follow this example.

Este es el horario de Miguel. En la primera hora, Miguel tiene la clase de matemáticas. Es su clase favorita. El Sr. Turka enseña la clase. En la segunda hora, Miguel tiene el español con la Sra. Schipani. Es una clase interesante. En la tercera hora, la Sra. Modico enseña la clase de inglés. El inglés es fácil. Miguel tiene la clase de ciencias sociales en la cuarta hora. Es una clase aburrida. Miguel tiene el Sr. Makellin para la clase de ciencias sociales. Por fin, Miguel tiene la clase de lectura. Es una clase difícil. La Srta. Jones enseña la clase.

Ejercicio 2.10b.
1. Juan acaba de caminar el perro.
2. Roberto y Diana acaban de mirar la televisión.
3. Yo acabo de hacer la tarea.
4. Nosotros acabamos de hablar por teléfono.
5. Tú acabas de comer un sándwich.

Ejercicio 2.10c.
1. En el salón de clases, les faltan los lápices.
2. En el casillero, me falta el libro.
3. En el gimnasio, le falta la ropa.
4. En la oficina, le falta la bandera.
5. En la cafetería (el comedor), te falta el almuerzo/la comida.

Ejercicio 2.10d.
1. Drop the -ar, -er, or -ir; add -ado to -ar verbs and -ido to -er or -ir verbs.
2. The present perfect tense is formed with two parts: the conjugated form of the verb "haber" and the past participle.
3. You can use the past participle as an adjective to modify a noun. You can express temporary state of being by preceding the past participle with a conjugated form of "estar."
4. A root word is the basic element from which the word has meaning. It is the foundation of the word.
5. Any of the following:

Abrir	to open	abierto	opened
Cubrir	to cover	cubierto	covered
Decir	to say, to tell	dicho	said, told
Describir	to describe	descri(p)	to described
Escribir	to write	escrito	written
Freír	to fry	frito	fried
Hacer	to do, to make	hecho	done, made
Imprimir	to print	impreso	printed
Ir	to go	ido	gone
Morir	to die	muerto	dead
Poner	to put, to place	puesto	put, placed
Resolver	to resolve	resuelto	resolved
Romper	to break	roto	broken
Satisfacer	to satisfy	satisfecho	satisfied
Ver	to see	visto	seen
Volver	to return	vuelto	returned

Section 3.1

Ejercicio 3.1a.

From left to right, top to bottom
Las uvas
El aguacate
La fresa
El arándano
La frambuesa
El limón
La cereza
El melocotón
La pera
La mora
La toronja/el pomelo
La sandía
La naranja
La piña
La manzana

Ejercicio 3.1b.

1. El albaricoque = apricot
2. La oliva = olive
3. El aguacate = avocado
4. El plátano = banana/plantain
5. El tomate = tomato
6. La frambuesa = raspberry
7. El coco = coconut
8. El mango = mango
9. La guava = guava
10. La papaya = papaya

Ejercicio 3.1c.

Answers may vary, but here are some possibilities.
1. Me gustan _____.
2. No me gustan _____.
3. Sí, me gustan las cerezas. O... No, no me gustan las cerezas.
4. Sí, me gustan las frambuesas y las moras. O... No, no me gustan.
5. Me gusta más _____.
6. Mi fruta favorita es _____.

Ejercicio 3.1d.

From left to right, top to bottom
La lechuga
El pimiento
La patata
El pepino
El champiñón
El elote, el choclo
La calabaza
El espárrago
La zanahoria
El maíz
El rábano
El brócoli
El apio
La berenjena
Los frijoles, las judías

Ejercicio 3.1e.

```
K  C  I  W  O  N  C  K  K  V  M  P  A  C  D
B  O  W  O  Z  K  R  O  P  S  Z  C  W  W  W
B  L  F  I  N  C  M  O  U  B  A  W  Y  O  U
X  D  D  B  A  G  N  L  L  N  Z  C  F  S  U
K  E  Y  A  B  Q  Q  X  I  F  A  J  L  J  S
B  B  Z  U  R  K  M  P  N  L  I  C  V  K  Q
K  R  H  C  A  P  S  Q  A  Q  K  L  A  T  J
B  Ú  P  L  G  E  D  B  M  I  S  L  O  N  Z
O  C  Q  A  O  G  A  R  R  Á  P  S  E  C  A
J  E  N  S  L  C  C  D  Q  A  I  O  F  E  J
Q  L  U  A  Í  K  H  T  H  K  W  H  F  I  O
D  A  O  N  B  H  Q  Y  D  S  G  X  H  M  Q
T  S  U  Y  L  O  A  E  M  A  Y  W  P  M  M
L  E  N  T  E  J  A  V  D  V  X  L  U  L  H
O  Y  X  M  S  P  S  D  Y  R  P  G  I  O  C
```

Ejercicio 3.1f.

Answers may vary, but here are some possibilities.

1. Prefiero _____.
2. Cinco verduras que como son: _____.
3. Las verduras que como son _____.
4. Me gusta más _____.
5. Sí, tengo que comer las verduras y los vegetales durante las comidas completas en casa.

Section 3.2

Ejercicio 3.2a.

Pictures should be of the following:

1. Meatloaf
2. Eggs and bacon
3. Fried chicken
4. A hamburger and 2 hotdogs
5. Sausage
6. Rabbit stew

Ejercicio 3.2b.

Answers will vary.

Ejercicio 3.2c.

1. Me gustaría el filete en su punto.
2. Me gusta la ternera.
3. No me gustan los huevos.
4. Quisiera un sándwich de chorizo.
5. No me gusta nada la carne de cerdo.

Ejercicio 3.2d.

You should have circled the following:

1. b, c, d
2. a, b, d
3. a, b, c
4. a, c, d
5. a, b, d
6. b, c, d

Ejercicio 3.2e.
1. c.
2. h.
3. b.
4. i.
5. g.
6. j.
7. d.
8. f.
9. a.
10. e.

Ejercicio 3.2f.
Review the vocabulary lists for the answers to the six categories.

Section 3.3

Ejercicio 3.3a.
1. el arroz
2. el panecillo
3. la tortilla
4. las patatas fritas
5. los espaguetis

Ejercicio 3.3b.
The list in the boxes will vary according to the reader's personal preference.

Ejercicio 3.3c.
1. Mi pizza favorita es _____.
2. Como los carbohidratos _____.
3. Como _____ rebanada/s de pan.
4. Prefiero _____.
5. Los italianos comen la pasta y los espaguetis.

Ejercicio 3.3d.
Across
1. caramelo
3. dulces
Down
1. comida basura
2. pastel
4. chupachups

Ejercicio 3.3e.
En la foto hay el pan tostado, los panqueques, una torta de chocolate, las galletas, y el biscocho.

Section 3.4

Ejercicio 3.4a.
1. B.
2. A.
3. B
4. B.
5. A.
6. A./B.
7. B.
8. B.
9. A.
10. A.

Ejercicio 3.4b.
Preferences will vary, but all sentences should begin with "prefiero."

Ejercicio 3.4c.
1. prefiero
2. prefieres
3. prefiere
4. prefieren
5. preferimos

Ejercicio 3.4d.
1. las palomitas
2. la fruta seca
3. el queso/ los quesos
4. las olives
5. la paleta helada
6. la chocolatina

Ejercicio 3.4e.
1. Mis tentempiés favoritos son las frutas secas y las nueces.
2. ¿En qué vas a picar?
3. Voy a tomar una merienda.
4. Voy a coger las palomitas de picar.
5. Me encanta comer las paletas heladas.

Section 3.5

Ejercicio 3.5a.

1. la mostaza, la salsa de tomate
2. la salsa picante
3. el aderezo para ensaladas
4. la mayonesa, la sal, la pimienta
5. el pico de gallo, la salsa

Ejercicio 3.5b.
1. vinagre
2. pimienta
3. mostaza
4. sal
5. mayonesa
6. aceite de oliva

Ejercicio 3.5c.
1. ¿Bebes el té helado?
2. ¿Con qué frecuencia bebes los refrescos?
3. ¿Usas el azúcar en el café?
4. ¿Qué prefieres: la coca-cola o la coca-cola de dieta?
5. ¿Te gustan los churros y el chocolate?

Ejercicio 3.5d.
Answers will vary.

Section 3.6

Ejercicio 3.6a.
1. saladas
2. dulces
3. agrio, amargo
4. sabor
5. picantes

Ejercicio 3.6b.
1. El agua está tibia.
2. El puré de patatas es soso.
3. Las palomitas son mantecosas.
4. El té está frío.
5. El bistec es muy sabroso.

Ejercicio 3.6c.
1. ¡Qué asco!
2. ¡Qué asco!
3. ¡Qué rico!
4. ¡Qué asco!
5. ¡Qué asco!

Ejercicio 3.6d.
1. La clase es interesantísima.
2. La comida es riquísima.
3. Las chicas son buenísimas.
4. Los churros son sabrosísimos.

Section 3.7

Ejercicio 3.7a.
1. Acabo de comer 4 hamburguesas; como como una __VACA_____.
2. Voy a comer porque __TENGO_____ mucha hambre.
3. Soy de __BUEN_____ comer.
4. Bebo el agua porque tengo __SED_____.
5. ¿Qué __HAY_____de comer?

Ejercicio 3.7b.
1. Tiene mucha hambre.
2. Voy a comer como una vaca.
3. ¿Qué hay de comer?
4. Es de buen comer.
5. Tienen mucha sed.

Ejercicio 3.7c.
Answers will vary.

Ejercicio 3.7d.
1. B., C.
2. B.
3. A.
4. A.
5. C.

Ejercicio 3.7e.
Para la cena, como el bistec, el puré de patatas, y los guisantes.
Para el desayuno, como el jamón, las salchichas, el tocino, los huevos, las fresas, y un bollo (un bizcocho).
Para el almuerzo, como una hamburguesa con queso, un perrito caliente, unas patatas fritas, y un refresco.

Section 3.8

Ejercicio 3.8a.
El tenedor   Fork
El cuchillo   Knife
La cuchara   Spoon
El vaso   Glass
La taza   Cup
El platillo   Saucer
El tazón   Bowl
El plato   Plate
La servilleta   Napkin

Ejercicio 3.8b.
Answers may vary, but here are some possibilities.
1. La servilleta está a la izquierda del tenedor.
2. El plato está entre el tenedor y el cuchillo.
3. El cuchillo está a la derecha del plato.
4. El platillo está debajo de la taza.
5. La taza está encima del platillo.

Ejercicio 3.8c.
1. el cuchillo → Se usa el cuchillo para cortar la carne.
2. el tazón → Se usa el tazón para la sopa y el cereal.
3. el tenedor → Se usa el tenedor para comer.
4. el vaso → Se usa el vaso para beber.
5. la cuchara → Se usa la cuchara para la sopa y el cereal.

Ejercicio 3.8d.
1. La comida española
2. La comida española
3. La comida mexicana
4. La comida mexicana
5. La comida española o la comida mexicana – This depends on whether the word means an omelet or round flat- bread.

Ejercicio 3.8e.
Answers will vary. Check answers with the lesson.

Section 3.9

Ejercicio 3.9a.
Answers will vary. It is advisable to check previous vocabulary lists to align food with categories.

Ejercicio 3.9b.
1. f.
2. a.
3. e.
4. d.
5. a.
6. c.
7. f.
8. b.
9. b.
10. d.

Ejercicio 3.9c.
1. los granos- 6 onzas
2. las frutas – 2 tazas
3. las carnes – 5.5 onzas
4. las verduras – 2. 5 onzas
5. los productos lácteos – 3 tazas

Ejercicio 3.9d.
Answers may vary but should begin with the following statements.
Debes comsumir _____.
Debes limitar _____.

Ejercicio 3.9e.
1. Yo ___DEBO_____ limitar las grasas.
2. Normalmente, no __CONSUMO_____ mucho pan.
3. ¿ __LIMITAS___ tú las grasas?
4. Mi amiga no ___COME_____ la comida buena.
5. Debo ___CONSUMIR_____ 2 tazas de frutas.

Section 3.10

Ejercicio 3.10a.

Las Frutas	**Las Verduras**	**Los Granos**
La toronja	El pepino	La harina
La naranja	La zanahoria	El panecillo
La cereza	El champiñón	El arroz
El albaricoque	El elote	La cebolla

Las grasas	**Los Productos Lácteos**	**Las Carnes y Frijoles Y los azucares**
La mantequilla	La leche	La soja
El jarabe de arce	El helado	El atún
El caramelo	El pudín	La chuleta
Los dulces	El queso de untar	La chuleta
		El cangrejo
		El pollo
		El pastel de carne
		Los frijoles

Ejercicio 3.10b.
    Answers will vary.

Ejercicio 3.10c.
    Para la cena, normalmente como el pollo al horno. También, tengo una verdura como las judías verdes con mantequilla. Preparo el puré de patatas con mantequilla. Son muy sabrosos. También, me gusta comer el postre como el helado o la torta de chocolate con la nata montada. Los postres son riquísimos y buenísimos. Mi familia y yo cenamos juntos.

Ejercicio 3.10d.
    Para el almuerzo, come un sándwich y una manzana. La comida es sabrosa. Tiene hambre. Debe limitar beber los refrescos.

Section 4.1

Ejercicio 4.1a.
    1. h
    2. b
    3. a
    4. i
    5. d
    6. g
    7. e
    8. f
    9. c

Ejercicio 4.1b.
    En el armario hay unos vestidos, unas camisas, unos suéteres, y unos pantalones.

Ejercicio 4.1c.
    The body should have a tank top, shorts, a sweatshirt, and sneakers.

Ejercicio 4.1d.
    1. llevo
    2. llevamos
    3. llevan
    4. llevas
    5. lleva

Ejercicio 4.1e.
    1. vestirme
    2. me visto
    3. se visten
    4. te vistes
    5. se visten

Ejercicio 4.1f.
    1. What are you wearing today?
    2. I am going to wear a sweatshirt and sweat pants.
    3. At what time are you going to get dressed?
    4. I am getting dressed at 8:00.
    5. The girls wear turtlenecks and pants.

Section 4.2

Ejercicio 4.2a.
1.   Juan is wearing a hat.
2.   Magda is wearing pants, a poncho and sandals.
3.   Paco is wearing a baseball cap.
4.   Rafaela is wearing jeans, a sweater, gloves and a scarf.

Ejercicio 4.2b.
1.   C
2.   A, C
3.   B
4.   A, B
5.   A, B
6.   A, C

Ejercicio 4.2c.
1.   las bragas, las tangas, la ropa interior, y el sostén, o el sujetador
2.   la ropa interior larga
3.   los calzoncillos
4.   las medias, las pantimedias (medias panty), y una combinación
5.   los calcetines
6.   los pijamas

Ejercicio 4.2d.
1.   Picture should be of boxers/briefs.
2.   Picture should be of pajamas.
3.   Picture should be of tights.
4.   Picture should be of long underwear.

Ejercicio 4.2e.
1.   d
2.   b
3.   e
4.   c
5.   a

Section 4.3

Ejercicio 4.3a.
1.   las pulseras
2.   los aretes, los pendientes
3.   los anillos
4.   los collares
5.   La cinta para el pelo
6.   Las pinzas, Las hebillas

Ejercicio 4.3b.
1.   Prefiero….
2.   Sí, me gustan los anillos nasales. No, no me gustan los anillos nasales.
3.   Sí, llevo los complementos diarios. No, no llevo los complementos diarios.
4.   Llevo….
5.   Sí, uso un cinturón cuando llevo pantalones. No, no uso un cinturón.

Ejercicio 4.3c.
1. verde
2. rojo
3. amarillo
4. violeta/morado
5. azul
6. café/marrón
7. negro y blanco
8. anaranjado

Ejercicio 4.3d.
1. Es de color rosado claro.
2. Mi color favorito es morado oscuro.
3. No me gusta el color verde.
4. ¿Te gustan el color amarillo?
5. ¿Es tu color favorito anaranjado?

Section 4.4

Ejercicio 4.4a.
1. ¿De qué color es la camisa?
2. ¿De qué color es la falda?
3. ¿De qué color es la chaqueta?
4. ¿De qué color son la bufanda y los guantes?

Ejercicio 4.4b.
1. El paraguas es amarillo. Or... Es un paraguas amarillo.
2. Las zapatillas de tenis son blancas. Or... Son unas zapatillas de tenis blancas.
3. La sudadera es roja. Or... Es una sudadera roja.
4. El traje es negro. Or... Es un traje negro.
5. El vestido es azul. Or... Es un vestido azul.

Ejercicio 4.4c.

Orange	→ la naranja	→ el color de naranja	→ orange-colored
Lime	→ la lima	→ el color de lima	→ lime-colored
Grape	→ la uva	→ el color de uva	→ grape-colored
Sand	→ la arena	→ el color de arena	→ sand-colored
Emerald	→ la esmeralda	→ el color de esmeralda	→ emerald-colored

Ejercicio 4.4d.
1. a
2. b
3. b, c
4. a, b, c, d
5. a, b, c, d

Ejercicio 4.4e.

```
O J I K H I O Q W W H O A Z K
A L K V O E U C E I I V U D G
K L E R D L H X X A J I N U F
K S E P S N N C W N G Y Ó L T
D U E A O F Q I F Q L P D N W
C U T D R I P H M D N R O B F
W B V K A G C K K Z U I G O B
G C B O X V L R Y T D F L Y S
P Z F J P F A E E Q M I A L W
T U D K V Z N N L T N Y Z T M
D S P I E L A V U O X W L Y Q
B O P W E M J Y T E B X D R C
S G W F L B Q M G F Y L T S N
P V D N B J X N Q K U V U R Y
B K Z R V G K D T Y D O T J C
```

Ejercicio 4.4f.
1. ¿Es la camisa de rayón?
2. ¿Llevas la ropa de piel y de cuero?
3. ¿Te gustan los pijamas de algodón?
4. ¿Llevas el terciopelo?
5. ¿Prefiere la fábrica natural o sintética?

Section 4.5

Ejercicio 4.5a.
The pictures should reflect these patterns (from left to right, top to bottom)
Paisley, floral, striped
Animal print, polka dots, plaid

Ejercicio 4.5b.
1. e
2. d
3. a
4. b
5. c

Ejercicio 4.5c.
La chica es morena con una coleta. Es guapa. Lleva un jersey de cisne en beige, un cinturón, y una falda a cuadros.

Ejercicio 4.5d.
Answers will vary.

Ejercicio 4.5e.
1. Halter tops are in style.
2. A romantic look could include a halter top and a long skirt.
3. Miniskirts and mini dresses are in style.
4. The mod look can be bright solid colors, no patterns or prints.

Ejercicio 4.5f.
1. Tengo una camisa amarilla con cuello vuelto desbocado.
2. Quiero una camisa de vestir de color azul con botones blancos.
3. Tiene que comprar una camisa roja sin mangas para la escuela.
4. La madre necesita comprar las zapatillas de tenis con cinta Velcro para su hijo.
5. Me gustan los suéteres negros con cuellos redondos más que los suéteres negros con cuellos cuadrados.

Section 4.6

Ejercicio 4.6a.

BAD FIT	NEUTRAL	GOOD FIT
Mal	Muy	Bien
Grande	Demasiado	Perfecto
Chico	Bastante	
Largo	Suficiente	
Corto		
Ancho		
Flojo		
Estrecho		
Apretado		
Arrugado		

Ejercicio 4.6b.
1. Esta camisa sin mangas está perfecta.
2. Estos pantalones están muy apretados.
3. Este vestido está demasiado flojo.
4. Este sombrero está muy mal.
5. Este traje está arrugado.

Ejercicio 4.6c.
Answers will vary.

Ejercicio 4.6d.
1. Yes
2. No
3. No
4. No
5. Yes

Section 4.7

Ejercicio 4.7a.
talla extra pequeña
talla pequeña
talla mediana
talla grande
talla extra grande

Ejercicio 4.7b.
Answers will vary by person but should follow the format below.
Llevo....

Ejercicio 4.7c.
1. True
2. True
3. True
4. True

Ejercicio 4.7d.
Answers will vary.

Section 4.8

Ejercicio 4.8a.
Tienda de lujo
Tienda de moda
Tienda de liquidaciones
Mercado al aire libre
Almacén
Centro comercial
Hidden phrase: El corte inglés

Ejercicio 4.8b.
1. Compro los juegos en la juguetería.
2. Voy a la sección electrodomésticos.
3. Voy de compras en la sección _____ (answers will vary).
4. La ropa está en la sección moda.
5. Hay relojes.

Ejercicio 4.8c.
Answers will vary. Check your vocabulary list.

Ejercicio 4.8d.
La clienta:	¿Es Ud. la vendedora de menaje?
La vendedora:	Sí, señora. ¿En qué puedo servirle?
La clienta:	¿Está a la __VENTA____ esta sartén en color amarillo?
La vendedora:	Hay una gran __PROMOCIóN_____ de ventas con muchas rebajas. La sartén tiene el precio habitual de 25 euros. Pero, el precio oferta con el descuento al menos de 50 porcentaje ahora está 12.50 __EUROS___. Es un precio bajísimo, ¿no?
La clienta:	Sí, mujer. Con los precios tan bajos, es mi oportunidad renovar mis accesorios de cocina.
La vendedora:	En la __VITRINA_____ hay más colores y diferentes tamaños.
La clienta:	Quiero comprar todos tamaños. ¿Cuánto cuesta con el PTA?
La vendedora:	El precio oferta con el impuesto es 17.82 cada uno.
La clienta:	___ES___ una ganga.
La vendedora:	Pienso que sí también.
La clienta:	Necesito un recibo de __VENTA_____.
La vendedora:	Claro, no problema.
La clienta:	Gracias.
La vendedora:	Y gracias a Ud.

Ejercicio 4.8e.

La clienta:	Are you the kitchenware sales clerk?
La vendedora:	Yes, ma'am, how can I help you?
La clienta:	Is this yellow frying pan on sale?
La vendedora:	There is a big sale with lots of sale items. The frying pan is normally 25 euros. But, the sale price with the 50% discount now is 12.50 euros. It's a really low price, isn't it?
La clienta:	Yes, woman. With the prices this low, it is my chance to update my kitchenware.
La vendedora:	In the case there are more colors and different sizes.
La clienta:	I want to buy all of the sizes. How much is it with the tax?
La vendedora:	The sales price with the tax is 17.82 each.
La clienta:	It's a bargain.
La vendedora:	I think so, too.
La clienta:	I need a receipt.
La vendedora:	Sure, no problem.
La clienta:	Thanks.
La vendedora:	Thank you, too.

Section 4.9

Ejercicio 4.9a.
1. Ellos piden los menús.
2. Pruebo la ropa.
3. Pide algo cada día.
4. Podemos ir.
5. No puedo comprar la camisa.

Ejercicio 4.9b.
1. Nosotros pedimos muchas cosas.
2. Ella prueba el vestido en el vestidor.
3. Vosotros podéis ayudarme.
4. ¿Puedes venir conmigo? - CORRECT
5. Pierde toda la moneda.

Ejercicio 4.9c.
1. ¿Puedes traerme otro tamaño?
2. No está de moda.
3. ¿Como me lo veo?
4. ¿Puedo ayudar en algo?/¿Qué desea?
5. No me queda bien.

Ejercicio 4.9d.
Answers will vary. Check vocabulary with list.

Section 4.10

Ejercicio 4.10a.
1. La bolsa blanca
2. Los pantalones a rayas
3. La chaqueta a lana
4. Los pijamas de algodón
5. El traje de baño a lunares rojos

Ejercicio 4.10b.

La chica rubia lleva una falda a raya con una blusa negra.

La chica morena lleva los pantalones de color de beige y una camisa de vestir blanca con mangas cortas.

Ejercicio 4.10c.

Voy a ir de compras. Llevo una camisa en talla pequeña. Me gusta la camisa y me queda bien.

Ejercicio 4.10d.
1. E.
2. F.
3. C.
4. D.
5. B.
6. G.
7. A.

INDEX

I